Praise for *What's Mom Still Got To Do With It?*

"From the first page, Ilana Tolpin Levitt draws the reader in with her poignant and insightful perspective of how family dynamics, particularly the conscious and subconscious aspects of the mother/daughter relationship, impact a career path and a fulfilled life. It truly is a must read for anyone who needs guidance and helpful advice from an experienced professional."

-Judge Patricia DiMango, *HOT BENCH,* a syndicated TV court program.

"*What's Mom Still Got To Do With It* is an important book for any woman who is beginning a career, is unhappy in her work, is changing careers, or simply wants to know herself better, both in the workplace and in her life. Ms. Levitt knows whereof she speaks, having worked with her mother and many women on the mother-daughter relationship, as well as being a career counselor herself. Putting the not so obvious 2 + 2 together (mothers + careers) gives all women a chance to stand up in their own truth, letting go of old messages (conscious and unconscious) that still define them, even in the workplace. And for the generations of women who are in the workforce now, this promise of being freed from limiting messages is a promise of better work outcomes and better all around mental health. It's also a great "how to" book, with tips that will serve you well, no matter which daughter type you might be. Thank you, Ilana, for carrying forward the important work of learning to be fully adult women, fully equal adults with our mothers and adult daughters and fully capable members of the work world."

-Dr. Dorothy Firman, co-author with her mother of *Daughters & Mothers: Making it Work* and other books including: *Chicken Soup for the Mother & Daughter Soul;* B*race for Impact: Miracle on the Hudson Survivors share their Stories of Near Death and Hope for a New Life*; and most recently *Engaging Life: Living*

D1416720

"All women will find many gems of insights within these pages. Drawing on years of practical application, this book contains a unique perspective never before addressed: how our relationships with our mothers affect our career choices. If you want to make life and career decisions with more intention, definitely add this to your list of key resources!"
Carol Vecchio, Life Design & Career Counselor and author of *The Time Between Dreams.*

"As a mindfulness coach who works with executive women, I have seen firsthand how women view themselves through the eyes of their mothers. Left unchecked, these patterns can persist throughout one's career. *What's Mom Still Got To Do With It* challenges us to pay attention to how we show up at work without assigning blame or judgment. Ilana draws on decades of career counseling to provide knowledgeable insight and practical tips, wrapped in a warm hug. I love this book and am going to keep plenty of copies on hand to give to my clients."
Tracy L Fink, Executive Women's Leadership and Mindfulness Coach.

"I love this book and this topic! *What's Mom Still Got To Do With It* is instantly engaging and bursting with vivid, relatable descriptions of women and their career challenges. Ilana offers practical, concrete steps to career change and professional growth. Every mother and adult daughter will benefit from this developmental, introspective, and unique path to self-discovery, career choice and success."
Dr. Lauren Saler, Psy.D, New York-based Clinical Psychologist.

What's Mom Still Got To Do With It?

Breathe New Life into Your Career by Understanding Your
Mother-Daughter Relationship

Ilana Tolpin Levitt, M.A., M.Ed.
In collaboration with Annie Wong

This is a work of nonfiction. Except for those who have given permission
to appear in this book, all names and identifying details and stories in this
book have been changed. In some instances, composite accounts have
been created based on my professional expertise.

Printed in the United States of America

Cover designed by Andrew Chin

Photo by Robert Fazio, Jr.

First Edition: January 2017

ISBN: 978-0-9984106-0-9 (print), 978-0-9984106-1-6 (e-book)

www.whatsmomthebook.com

10 9 8 7 6 5 4 3 2 1

This book is dedicated to all women, grandmothers, mothers and daughters alike, as we continue to define our imprint in the working world.

Table of Contents

"A daughter is a mother's gender partner, her closest ally in the family confederacy, an extension of herself. And mothers are their daughters' role models, their biological and emotional road map, the arbiter of all their relationships."

-Victoria Secunda

Introduction

"From a young age, I had a pretty good idea of what I wanted to do with my life. I guess it didn't hurt to see my mom juggling family and work."

"I didn't know what I wanted to be when I was growing up. I just knew I didn't want to be like my mother."

"My mom didn't have many career opportunities but she sacrificed so much to make sure that I went to college and have a career."

"I'm great at my job but why does it always seem like I've got the lion's share of the work?"

The comments above are commonplace -- you hear them all the time from women everywhere. You may even have said them yourself. What you may not have considered is that your mom had a lot to do with how you make decisions about work. It's odd, isn't it? We don't dispute the depth of our mother's influence in our everyday lives, but when it comes to the workplace we draw an invisible line that we think keeps Mom out. It doesn't. In each and every one of us, we carry the lessons our mothers taught us. We will continually use her as a reference on what to do and how to react in all facets of our lives. Whether we're aware of it or not, we'll depend on her opinion to affirm that our choices were "right." She was one of our first and most important role models -- maybe in a good way and maybe in a bad way, but isn't that true of most people who touch our lives? Her words, experiences, and opportunities will echo in our subconscious minds in meaningful, yet largely unexplored ways. In addition to Mom being a role model in our personal and professional lives, we still care deeply about what she thinks of the choices we make, even if we don't want to care. Her criticism might just come from a simple look in response to your news about taking an unusual job, spending an exorbitant (perhaps even unnecessary?) amount of money on graduate school, or, moving abroad for a few years. This book starts the process of discovering how her words, experiences, opportunities, and her very being have impacted you in your professional life.

In the United States, women face increasing opportunities to pursue their career ambitions and make significant contributions in fields that used to be accessible only to men. However, despite the change in women's roles in society, it's still not accurate to say that men and women have equal experiences in the workplace. While much research has documented the differences between men's and women's careers and roles in the workplace, very few studies explore these differences from the perspective of this book – how our mothers impacted our professional lives.

While I may not remember how my Mom took care of me when I was a baby, I can use our talks later in life to piece together a general idea of how she took care of me when I could remember, and, I can glean a sense of how she cared for me by looking at how I take care of my own children now. She fed me, kept me warm, and comforted me when I was upset or in pain. She taught me what was right and what was wrong. She let me know when it was okay for me to complain and when I had to "grin and bear it." I learned what made her tick, and what would bring out that critical look in her eyes. Almost all of my limited memories before I was four or five years old involved my mom in some capacity. And while dads, brothers or sisters, grandmas and grandpas, aunts, uncles, and other people also may have featured prominently, for now we're just focusing on moms. Mom was my constant, and she was probably yours too. Women have turned to, and continue to refer to, the lessons we learned from our mothers in not just the personal aspects of our lives but the professional ones as well. Mom is our first and most important role model, even if neither of you was aware of it.

In my own experience, as a little girl I was both awed, and maybe a little intimidated by, my mother, Leah. She was a strong woman. Like the proverbial little duckling, I followed her around the house, watching and wondering about all the things she was thinking about and doing. She went back to work when I was six, and I remember being happy when she was home. Sometimes I wouldn't say a word; I'd just stare at her, fascinated with how she spoke and behaved with other people who were not me. I recall being amazed by how she managed the house, her therapy clients, how she prepared for the holidays, even with the way she folded the laundry. When I was sick, she knew exactly which part on my back to rub to make me feel better; she knew when I was lying about brushing my teeth; and, she knew how to quell any whining or bad behavior with just the right words. When she was present and not too busy with her work, she was very tuned in to me and to my siblings.

My mother was not perfect, a conclusion I came to when I became a teenager. Her requests could elicit from me all sorts of irrational, uncalled-for irritation. Deep down, I was afraid she was judging me if she didn't like my friends or my choice of weekend activities. My responses, whether expressed or not, usually fell into a few general categories: "Leave me alone"; "I know what I'm doing"; "I don't need help"; or "I don't need your approval." (But I actually really did need her approval.) In case you're wondering, this is a healthy process for all adolescent girls to go through. It's the start of separation, when young women realize they are not exactly like their mothers, and that Mom isn't perfect. When I was old enough to start seriously thinking about choosing a career, I admired that my mom was a psychoanalyst, but I never considered becoming a psychoanalyst or psychotherapist as a career goal for myself. As it turns out, though, this apple did not fall far from the tree...

It wasn't until I had graduated from college and after I started pursuing my career in psychology and counseling that I re-connected with and to my mother, no longer as child-to-mother, but woman-to-woman. Leah was an introverted, Belgian-born woman who escaped the horrors of the Holocaust and came to the United States when she was nine years old. She became a psychoanalyst and specialist in group work. I found ways to emulate my mother's strengths while developing a style that was distinct and different. As her American-born daughter, I graduated from Columbia University with degrees in Counseling and Organizational Psychology. While Mom focused on general counseling, I specialized in career counseling. Thanks to her, it never seemed like an insurmountable challenge for me to start my own private practice right out of school. After all, I watched her manage her own successful practice while raising a family at the same time. It was a natural step for me to do the same.

It's been 26 years since I started practicing as a career counselor. At the start, I wasn't viewing many of the issues my clients were bringing to me through the daughter-mother lens. Somewhere along the way, however, I realized there was something significant about this unique dynamic, and that when my clients were able to unlock the secrets to the special relationships with their moms, they were also able to move on to more satisfying careers that made them happier. Because Mom was also a trained counselor, we talked about the mother-daughter dynamic early on in my career. It might have been what gave us the impetus to lead workshops for mothers and daughters in the New York and New Jersey metropolitan areas, from 1989 to 2003. My mother and I could run these mother-daughter workshops because I chose a career path that was similar to hers. We could each bring our own special elements into the workshops, which allowed women to open doors in their relationships with their mothers or daughters, making room for expansive progress.

During those workshops, mothers and daughters, sometimes three generations within the same family, would attend together to try to strengthen, understand, and repair their links with each other. We witnessed and confirmed the importance of a mother's influence on her daughter's career path and work issues. Through the real-life experiences of these multi-generational workshops and my own private practice, I began to see five basic types of mother-daughter relationships. Each of them have a distinct impact on a daughter's future career. After charting over 100 stories, five types of daughters emerged. These are not meant to be rigid definitions; they have somewhat loose boundaries, so women may identify with more than one type at any given time, or even transition from one to another in their adult lives. One woman may even identify with multiple types simultaneously. Not everyone may feel like they fit neatly into one daughter type, but if you dig deeply enough, you'll find yourself connecting with some themes or elements from at least one type. Also, keep in mind that, when we pass major milestones over time, when we achieve or fall short of certain goals, or when our family constellations change, our daughter type can also change. In the following pages, I'll summarize each type and then elaborate on each in individual chapters.

Ivy Daughter

At a young age, she needed more than her mother would, or could, give her. She was left wanting more. As an adult, she may challenge authority, or try to control circumstances beyond her reach and even strive to hide a sweet, affectionate nature. Veronica is this type of daughter. She often has a reputation for being difficult at work. Although Veronica excelled at her job, when she was promoted to manager, her department became a revolving door and employees described her as an antagonistic micro-manager. She fared no better with the managers above her, who also found her difficult. Veronica believes that the people complaining about her at work were intimidated by her intelligence and ambition. She was unable to see how her own actions might have contributed to disciplinary action. Veronica's mother had been unable to overcome her own disappointments, and so she was unable to give Veronica the attention she wanted as a child.

You might be an Ivy daughter if you. . .

1. *Fight tooth and nail for a cause or a person you believe in.*
2. *Expect others to fight tooth and nail for you.*
3. *Seek unusual amounts of attention from bosses.*
4. *Are easily hurt by people who let you down.*
5. *Consider yourself to be a demanding boss.*
6. *Think that problems in your life are caused by others, not you.*

Maverick Daughter

Perhaps her mother held onto her too tightly. The Maverick daughter grows up but continues to rebel for the sake of rebelling. She may be loving or attention seeking in one moment, but in the next moment she wants to be left alone without apparent reason. A Maverick daughter is a perpetual teenager. Even though she has a Master's degree, 31-year-old Tonya struggles to pay her bills. As a freelance graphic designer, she has trouble actively seeking new clients and lags behind in billing her existing clients. Tonya's mother supplements her income; in fact, Tonya is reluctantly thinking of moving back home with her mother. Tonya's mother has career issues as well. To Tonya's dismay, her mother loves to claim that they are exactly alike.

You might be a Maverick daughter if you. . .

1. *Changed your career multiples times in the past few years.*
2. *Question your career choices.*

3. *Do the opposite of what your partner or boss tells you to do.*
4. *Want a close relationship with your mother but push her away.*
5. *Find your mother too controlling or judgmental about your choices.*
6. *Wish you had more of a career identity.*

Butterfly Daughter

Her mother may not have been a role model in terms of "career" but was otherwise supportive of her choices and growth. Because of this encouragement, the Butterfly Daughter is able to spread her wings and avail herself of opportunities that Mom never had. Despite her success, she remains insecure. Rosa is a successful radiologist with over 20 years of experience. Although she is well liked and respected by patients, peers, and other staff, she has been passed over for promotion many times. Her mother stayed at home to raise six children, and Rosa credits Mom with providing unwavering encouragement that helped her get through her toughest year in medical school.

You might be a Butterfly daughter if you/your...

1. *Mother had fewer career opportunities than you.*
2. *Mother encouraged you and made sacrifices so that you could advance further than she did.*
3. *Have secret doubts about your success.*
4. *Wish you had more of a role model at home for career success.*
5. *Are the first in your family to graduate from college.*
6. *May create your own glass ceiling at work.*

Copycat Daughter

Her mother had a successful career and was a role model who established a familiar path. Mother and daughter usually remain closely connected, even after separation, and the Copycat Daughter chooses to follow her mother's career path closely. Tasha followed in her mother's footsteps into the world of magazine publishing. Her mother focused on high fashion but the idea of placating divas was not something Tasha had any interest in doing. Despite her success, she often feels like she's trying to stack her achievements alongside her mother's accomplishments -- and when she surpasses her mother, she feels guilty.

You might be a Copycat Daughter if you...

1. *Are in the same general field as your mother.*
2. *Consider her to be a role model for your career.*
3. *Are often compared to your mother.*
4. *Are proud of and admire your mother.*
5. *Feel like you have big shoes to fill, career-wise.*

Bootstrap Daughter

The Bootstrap daughter is the "parentified" daughter who had to take care of things at home. She's had to pull herself up using her own bootstraps to get to where she is today. As an adult, however, she may still struggle with identifying a truly satisfying career. At 34, Sunny has a great job at a corporate office where she excels. Having a stable job is something that she's always appreciated, but she often wonders if she should have focused on a more creative career. Her mother immigrated to the United States from Korea and worked many low-wage, menial jobs. As a result, Sunny doesn't want to let her mother down and feels too responsible for her family to switch careers at this point in her life.

You might be a Bootstrap daughter if you/your...

1. *Had to take care of your mother when you were growing up.*
2. *Mother was addicted to alcohol or drugs.*
3. *Parents emigrated from another country and depended on you to serve as their translator.*

4. *Had to learn about cultural or social norms from your friends.*
5. *Were or are the caregiver in the family.*
6. *Feel like you carry a big weight of responsibility on your shoulders.*

It's an over-simplification and unfair to say that a woman's career issues boil down to her relationship with her mother. However, there is an undeniable link. When women find themselves stuck, sometimes the only way out is exploring the depths of their relationship with their mothers, and all the implicit and explicit messages they were taught in childhood about the world of work. Perhaps the most challenging task is for women to recognize that their mothers, like themselves, come with strengths and limitations. Even the mother who meets every one of her child's needs, may create a daughter who didn't learn how to do for herself.

What's Mom Still Got to Do With It? is a book for women who may not know why they are feeling lost at work and feeling isolated about it. It's also a book for women who have close relationships with their moms and recognize how the powerful bond has helped them to succeed. It's even possible (and probable) that your relationship, like most relationships, is a mixture of positive and negative experiences. My dream is to have the opportunity to help women through the exploration of the mother-daughter relationship as a means to get unstuck. For the past 26 years in my private practice, women have come to see me with an assortment of career problems that they want to resolve. It could be an inability to make decisions, lack of motivation, failure to communicate their value to employers, or unhealthy thoughts about their career (for instance, "No one's hiring" or "I'll do anything except what I'm doing now"). In terms of decision-making, there may be a lack of commitment or an anxiety to commit to anything. The range of issues is vast and can be very painful. Sometimes, women have too many good choices and can't narrow down their options, or they want coaching about how to navigate in the workplace.

This book has stories from real women living through their own challenges; it also provides powerful advice and tips for recognizing work obstacles -- why they're there and how to overcome them, so you can create a more meaningful life. Regardless of your age, it's never too late to understand the impact your mom had on your career.

While our mothers will always play a critical role in our lives, my goal for all of us is to be able to accept and incorporate the good aspects of the mother-daughter dynamic, reject what doesn't work, and truly discover our separate selves. When you've achieved this goal, you will not only find a better path in life, but you may also be able to connect or empathize more deeply with your mother in ways you never thought possible. The key to understanding past decisions that you regret, or problematic relationships at work, could well lie within this dynamic. Come along with me now to explore vitally important aspects of your past, consider your present realistically, and take wise actions for a more satisfying career in the future.

Chapter 1:

Daughters and Their Mothers

The fact of the matter is, people never forget the implicit and explicit lessons they learned in childhood. Experiences with and around their mothers are hardwired deep into the psyches of adult daughters. Our gender and our role models do influence the goals we set for ourselves, how we set them, and our reactions to situations and people along the way. This is neither a good or bad thing; it's simply one of the factors that makes up a person, like the color of your hair or the shape of your nose.

Louisa, for example, just turned 27 and was recently promoted to a Senior Paralegal position. She and her husband, Tony, also just found out she's pregnant with their first child. Louisa and Tony are ecstatic about the news, but their reactions are different. Tony is thinking about working harder and taking on more projects at his job so that he can get a promotion and ultimately save enough money to buy a house. Louisa, on the other hand, is consumed with questions that might be similar to yours, if you had a good job and you were also expecting. "Should I put aside my career and stay home to raise my child? What's more important: my job or my family?"

In Tony's and Louisa's situation, the differences are clear. There's no expectation that Tony needs to curtail any of his career pursuits with the presence of a new baby; in fact, he believes he needs to work more in order to adequately provide for his growing family. Louisa, on the other hand, is torn because she thinks career and child rearing are incompatible. It's not an uncommon assumption, particularly in some specific cultures. The questions that Louisa asks herself are tough, and there is no one-size-fits-all answer out there.

Fifty years ago, once a woman got married, she was expected to stop working, have children, and take care of the household. Twenty years ago, one of the more common beliefs was that women could manage a full-time job and be a full-time mother simultaneously. They were called "Super Moms." Today, women seem more inclined to acknowledge that the Super Mom model isn't necessarily the right answer after all. Louisa will undoubtedly reflect on how she was raised and the choices her mother made. Louisa's own mom tried to live up to the expectation of "having it all and doing it all." Do you know what Louisa actually saw? "She was just tired all the time," Louisa says of her mother. "She was constantly juggling the priorities and demands of her job and us. Sometimes, I felt bad for her -- because it didn't seem like Mom ever had time to do anything she ever wanted. She told me a few years ago that she didn't feel like she was focused enough on either one." Whatever Louisa's decision ends up being, she knows she doesn't want to be just like her mom. Because Louisa admires her mom, she might, nonetheless, feel like a failure if she doesn't try to have it all -- and do it all. There is no easy answer, but after exploring this important dynamic, we (and Louisa) may have a better understanding of why, or how, we make the decisions that we make.

Mothers' influences on their adult daughters extend beyond choosing whether or not to return to work full-time, part-time, or not at all after they've had children. Whether you or I realize it, we are consciously and unconsciously observing how our mothers dealt with work-related situations (Did she rise up through the ranks? Did she decide to start her own business?) This behavior influences how we choose or avoid particular professions, respond to stress at work, perform in leadership roles, and even how we interact with female bosses. Believe it or not, the mother-daughter dynamic plays a strong role in these seemingly unrelated matters. The adult mother-daughter relationship is unique and deep. It can be an easy camaraderie, antagonistic, suffocating, enriching, and baffling at various phases or all at the same time. It has the potential for the deepest mutuality and extreme, painful estrangement. Some adult daughters regard their mothers as one of their closest friends; other daughters have little or no contact with them. Whatever the relationship may be between you and your mom, this dynamic began developing the moment you were born, and will remain an intense and instrumental force in your life.

Marianne Walters writes in her book, *The Invisible Web*: "If mother is the cornerstone of family life, the mother-daughter relationship is the brick and mortar that holds them together." When a relationship is so powerful, it has the potential to enrich and to destroy. At the heart of the workshops I led with my mom, mothers and daughters sat across from each other in an attempt to understand one another. They were asked to describe the nature of their relationships metaphorically through colors, animals, and textures. We received a variety of responses -- from lovebirds and lions to snakes, chameleons, and giraffes in all shades of the rainbow. They said these relationships had textures like tweed, silk and sandpaper to illustrate the complexities between mother and daughter.

These bonds were explored more deeply when mothers and daughters opened up to one another in the presence of other mothers and daughters. Some mothers wanted to know why their daughters were pushing them away, while their daughters attempted to explain perceived slights or criticisms. Often mothers and daughters found comfort in seeing that there were others whose relationships weren't perfect. Society expects women to be close with their mothers. Because we created a safe space where these expectations were put aside, many women found our sessions healing, cathartic, and emotionally intense.

Today's adult daughters may resent the lack of choices their mothers had in the workplace, or that men had so many more opportunities back then. These feelings actually can spark conflict in the mother-daughter dynamic, through no fault of anyone. It's both wonderful and sad: never before have women had as many career avenues open to us, but, at the same time, we might feel lost in the face of all these opportunities. We may end up blaming our mothers, if they couldn't help us through an important decision-making process, or if they couldn't relate to the work issues we're going through. When this happens, I tell myself and others to be mindful that only in the last 50 years have there been advances in the women's liberation movement. Our moms, and their moms, and their moms' moms probably lived severely restricted lives. There were very few career options. In fact, the choice spectrum for many women included only mother, teacher, secretary, or nurse. Today, since women's work vistas are far more open, their career challenges can be drastically different than what their mothers and grandmothers experienced.

Still, despite the common assumption that we have outgrown our past experiences and our childhoods like a pair of baby shoes, the impressions that are formed in our early years flavor how we make our decisions every single day. This is true, whether we are fresh out of college, an established professional in her 40s, or approaching retirement. Since our mothers are so integral to how we developed, the answer to the question, *What's Mom Still Got to Do With It?*, is not merely a lot, but a huge amount. She was the primary caregiver for many women, and thus our role model for life and career. We can't, and shouldn't, discount the intensity of the mother-daughter relationship. It stays with us even when she is gone. Mom will always have a major impact on how we live our lives; our relationship with her may, to a certain extent, explain why and where we might get stuck. Whether we like it or not, our mothers are actually incorporated inside of us.

It's different for men. For most of history and throughout most of the world, we've lived in a male-dominated society. Even though this continues to be the case, the 21st century has provided women with more career opportunities, including choices traditionally enjoyed by men. Also, more women in the workforce today are gaining recognition for their innovation and leadership skills. But because of the relative recency of the women's movement, men have had an advantage in the workplace, as they have looked to their fathers and other male figures as role models. Women have not had the same advantages. On top of that, we continue to struggle with our roles inside and outside the home. These are new dilemmas that we approach instinctively, for better or worse, by referring back to how and what we saw our mothers do. It might take another generation or two to catch up emotionally to where women are in reality. We may be able to get into certain roles, but the question we haven't quite figured out the answer to is, "Are we comfortable being there?"

I wouldn't be surprised if many of you reading this book are nodding your heads at this moment. But for the skeptics out there, think about your reactions to the following: believing that you have surpassed or fallen short of your mother's dreams or career success; when you have consciously made the decision to be just like, or the opposite of, your mother; when you have to tell her you're moving across the country for an opportunity or quitting your job to become a stay-at-home mom; and consider how you get along with women bosses. If any of these situations evoked a strong reaction, positive or negative, it means that these are potential pressure points for you in your mother-daughter dynamic.

The Psychology Behind the Mother-Daughter Dynamic

What exactly makes the mother-daughter dynamic so intense? When a baby is born, mother and child form a strong, emotional bond. It can be exponentially more powerful between a mother and daughter because they are the same sex. The new mother can identify with her newborn daughter almost immediately, knowing (perhaps assuming) that as she gets older the daughter will likely go through life experiences similar to her mother's experiences. When this attachment exists between daughter and mother, a girl learns not only how to view the world around her, but also how to respond to it and feel safe in it. All of this happens before she's six years old! When we learn at such early stages in our lives, it's called preconscious memory; although we were too young to remember those lessons, they nonetheless impact us well into our adult lives.

As children, daughters copy their mothers' ways -- the way they walk, the way they speak, even the way they make the bed or put away clothes. There comes a time, though, when these daughters suddenly realize that they are not their mothers and instead of being afraid of this distinction, they feel a profound sense of liberation. This is how separation starts. At this stage, it's not unusual for daughters to create boundaries that put distance between themselves and their mothers. They may even go overboard and make pronounced declarations about how they're nothing like their moms. Though separation is a natural process for children, it can be difficult and even painful for mothers. It's hard not to take this personally!

Separation issues become prominent when girls reach their teenage years. While daughters are experiencing biological and social changes in adolescence, many of their mothers are entering their middle-of-life phase and are re-evaluating their roles at work and in the home. Girls are noticing changes in their bodies, and they seem more interested in, and influenced by, their friends rather than their parents. Moms may be going through menopause or may suddenly find they have more time for work and their personal lives now that their kids require less attention. Mothers and daughters with more intense levels of attachment and identification will experience greater difficulty in separation. How separation is handled and whether it is achieved in a healthy manner will not only affect their adult relationships but also how daughters approach potential conflicts in their adult lives, including career challenges.

To better understand the psychology of women's development, I'm going to explain two other important themes: identification and individuation. Identification is essentially when one person wholly imitates another person's actions, behaviors, and to a certain extent, their thoughts and feelings. To this day, even though I have my own established life, vestiges of this remain. For instance, when my son was young and took a bad fall on the sidewalk, I remember screaming, "Oopsa!" I had never said that word before in my life, but it was my mother's word, literally, coming out of my mouth. Annie, who helped me write this book, can't wear any new underwear without washing it first, as she had seen her mother do during her entire childhood. Both she and I have made traditions of our mothers' quirks. It wouldn't surprise me, if our moms learned them from their moms. Why does this happen? It's because we are our mothers' daughters. We internalized these quirks when we were young, through preconscious memory. They are inside of us.

Identification isn't a one-way street. At the same time that daughters are identifying with their mothers, their mothers are also doing the same with their daughters. It starts before the girl is born. When the daughter is just a fetus in her womb, the expectant mother imagines what her child will look like and what her interests will be. She may have a natural curiosity, and also hope that she and her daughter will share similar likes and dislikes. When the daughter is born and grows, her mother grows as well, and the experiences that the daughter goes through will resonate keenly with a mother's own past experiences. It may be problematic for a mother, if the daughter she fantasized about even before her birth turns out to be completely different from her.

You won't find the same intensity in a mother-son relationship for one simple reason: they are not the same sex. Mothers' expectations are very different for their sons than for their daughters. There is a greater cultural pressure for women to remain connected with their mothers throughout their lives. On the other hand, men are mocked and derided, if they appear too close to their mothers, often being labeled as a "mama's boy." Society judges mama's boys as more pathological and socially unacceptable than women who are close to their fathers (a "daddy's girl") or mothers. In fact, there is no label for a "mama's girl", because it is considered a normal part of the mother-daughter relationship. Little girls can stay identified with their mothers for a longer period of time than boys. There is no psychological need for daughters to separate from their mothers before puberty, but little boys are made to understand at an early age, that they are not like their moms. They separate much earlier, in order to identify with fathers or other male role models. In Chapter 7, we'll shed light on how other relationships within the family play a role in women's career and career blockages.

The other important psychological theme in women's development is individuation, a period of time when a daughter's memory, perception, and cognition develop. Individuation is an ongoing process, but during the preteen years, young girls realize who they are, separate from their parents. They are more aware of the world in which they live. External influences outside of the family begin to take on a more prominent role for pre-adolescent daughters. At this age, daughters are also more aware not only of the different roles people take on, but the differences and inequalities based on gender. For example, girls may observe their mothers getting up an hour earlier than their fathers to pack school lunches and get the children dressed and ready for the day. Then they see their mothers rushing home to make dinner, check homework, and spend time with the children. Daughters may conclude from these observations that adult women are expected to shoulder more of the household responsibilities and that fathers have a higher need to relax after work, even when both parents work equally long hours, or when Mom works even more. Individuation also involves daughters realizing that they are different from their mothers, as in how a teenaged Annie would disagree with her mother at the mall about a "nice" dress to wear to a school dance – she felt her mom's choices were "too frumpy," and Mom considered Annie's choices "too grown up."

Everyone goes through these psychological processes early in life: identification, separation, and individuation. The daughter grows up to become a person who is different from her mother, and these differences often challenge the mother-daughter dynamic. If the daughter looks more like her father, her mother may see this as an unconscious separation; some mothers may even see it as a betrayal. In middle school, I had to choose to study either Spanish or French to fulfill my language course requirements. I chose French because my mother spoke it fluently. At the time, I didn't know why I chose it other than the superficial reason that I liked the way the language sounded. Thinking about it now, I know part of the reason I selected French was to avoid potentially "betraying" my mom. She would not have felt betrayed, mind you; it was my personal fear of hurting her, or separating myself from her, that drove my decision. My brother, on the other hand, had an easier time choosing Spanish instead of French because it wasn't as personal a decision.

For you, signs of separation could have been equally minor yet significant decisions: choosing to enroll in the local college or going out of state; spending Spring Break at the beach instead of in a city; eating meat rather than being a vegetarian. Much of this is values-based. Often when daughters deviate from how their mothers expect (or hope) they will act or behave, it's not because they are intentionally trying to hurt their mothers. Regardless, their moms may view it as such because it is the daughter unconsciously choosing to move away from a previously shared identity. A mother may feel badly when this happens because she's used to her daughter feeling or behaving in the same way, and it may literally seem like her world is falling apart when her daughter moves in a different direction. This dynamic is true even for emotionally healthy women, so you can only imagine how complicated separation is for mothers who have their own psychological issues.

Patterns in the mother-daughter relationship are set from a very early age, with many factors contributing to it, such as each person's temperament, and their interactions with one another and with the other members of the family. As the daughter grows, both the ways and the intensity in which she and her mother attach, identify, and ultimately separate, greatly impact this very intimate, primary relationship.

Adult Daughters: What's Mom Still Got to Do With It?

Significant research illuminates the impact of early childhood attachment between a mother and her babies. This research shows that when the attachment between mother and daughter is compromised in early life (i.e., when a daughter doesn't get enough mothering), it can have lasting effects on an adult daughter's relationships, including those at work. When I first developed my daughtering model, I thought about how we carry our mothers inside of us, and how they did the same with their own mothers. In a similar fashion, we carry within ourselves the different versions of the daughters we are or were, too. There is still a small child and adolescent girl living inside all of us. It's a natural effect from the changing relationships we had with our moms throughout our lives -- from following her around, wanting to be just like her, doing things that differentiate ourselves from her, to empathizing/sympathizing with her and maybe even accepting our similarities (and differences).

The image of a nesting doll is perfect for illustrating the different daughters we are or can become. In my model, these nesting daughters are distinguished into five different types, based on two conditions: (1) the past or present mother-daughter dynamic; and (2) associated career issues. The nesting daughters model synthesizes the past quarter of a century that I've spent counseling clients, hearing women's stories, and identifying patterns in their relationships with their moms. Where do you fit in? Would you like to change your position for a happier work life? How can you do it? We'll explore these important issues more deeply in the next few chapters.

Chapter 2:

The Ivy Daughter

Veronica was the kind of employee many managers dreamed of hiring -- she was detail-oriented, asked questions, and was thorough about reporting her progress to her supervisors. She worked at a financial company and when her manager left, to her delight, she was promoted to replace her boss. In her new role, Veronica supervised two employees. That's when the trouble started. Both employees resigned within a year, and her department became known as the "revolving door" because of the high turnover rate. Exit interviews revealed that many of Veronica's former employees described her as "too much of a micromanager," "overly critical about mundane details," and, when overwhelmed, "unbearable and negative."

At the same time, Veronica had issues with her new boss, the General Manager of the company. Veronica wasn't as close with her new boss, as she'd been with her former supervisor. Suddenly, she felt she had to "compete" with five other people who also reported to the General Manager. She had trouble grasping the new dynamics at work. At a meeting with other senior managers present, Veronica made a joke about her supervisor's competency. Judging from the uncomfortable silence that followed, she thought perhaps it hadn't been received well. This was confirmed when her General Manager, Morgan, called her into her office an hour later and issued her a warning for insubordination. Veronica was stunned, but this quickly transformed into anger. She accused Morgan of "playing favorites" with the other managers, and of "picking on" Veronica for no good reason. Although Morgan denied it, Veronica didn't believe her. She began to view work as a political battlefield and felt it was necessary to have "allies" there. Veronica did this by sharing her negative views about Morgan and the company with others at the office.

Morgan was puzzled because Veronica's predecessor had spoken so highly of Veronica, and yet she was now creating so much internal conflict. Despite the trouble that came with managing Veronica, Morgan was reluctant to fire her because when Veronica focused on the work, she was great. Several high-performing employees who also reported up to Morgan complained to her about Veronica being overly critical and said they would be looking for new jobs elsewhere. When Morgan addressed this with Veronica, she replied that "letting them leave was a step in the right direction." Morgan had had enough. Veronica was issued a final ultimatum: she had to consult with a career coach or she would be in danger of losing her job. That's how Veronica was referred to me. It wasn't an auspicious beginning for deep discussion, but Veronica was clearly distressed and more than a little confused about why this was happening to her.

Sometimes, I think I worry about this type of daughter the most. Many Ivy daughters make a strong first impression; they are often described as ambitious, authoritative, and resilient. Before Veronica was promoted to her current manager position, her old boss valued Veronica's ability to confront difficult people and situations directly. This was viewed as an asset because Veronica's previous manager was more conflict-avoidant and would often leave these kinds of challenges for Veronica to handle. It was one of the reasons why the manager advocated for Veronica's promotion. The action was short sighted because the manager position also required more finesse and diplomacy than Veronica possessed. Employees who had not been consulted when Veronica was promoted, described her as a bully when it came to getting her way. They said she didn't know how to argue or persuade constructively. She did not approve of, and resented, many forms of dissension. One of her former direct-reports said: "If we deviated even a little bit, or, God forbid, thought there was a better approach, she could get nasty. She liked pointing out, more times than I can count, how the company practically begged her to take the manager job. In light of that, how could her subordinates possibly know better?"

Hard to believe, then, that hidden deep beneath this rough and tough exterior, Veronica was a vulnerable person who bruised easily. Growing up, she had a difficult relationship with her mom, Sarah. Veronica remembers clearly that Sarah always talked about her aspirations to be a ballerina. When Sarah was pregnant with Veronica, she gave up that dream at the insistence of her in-laws, to focus on family. Adding to Sarah's disappointment, Veronica's physical build differed from her own. "As a child, I had Dad's wide shoulders and hips," Veronica recalled. "I always think Mama and I might have got on easier, if I was tall and slim like her. When I was five years old, she forced me to take ballet lessons. That was a nightmare; I was a complete klutz, no matter how hard I practiced. Mama accused me of intentionally being bad at ballet, saying that I liked to spite her, ruin her day. Nothing I said or did made her believe otherwise of me." After her very last ballet class, Veronica felt immense relief, followed by guilt that she had "somehow let Mama down again."

Her father, Austin, was a financial advisor for wealthy clients, and their family was able to live very comfortably on his income alone. Veronica remembers her mom showing very little interest in work. Sarah claimed she'd rather be "bored to tears sitting at home than at a desk poring over dusty piles of paper." At a young age, Veronica knew not to broach the subject of Sarah returning to dance. It would place her mother in an "awful mood" for days. The only passion that Sarah seemed to have was traveling, often to see Veronica's maternal grandparents, who lived abroad. Sarah would be absent for months at a time, leaving Veronica to the care of her father, her paternal grandparents, and a nanny. Her mother's return was always a grand affair. Veronica could expect at least ten new outfits (that never fit her) and an abundance of other gifts. Sarah would hug her daughter and tell her how much she'd missed her. But, as Veronica puts it, "it never occurred to Mama, not even when I asked, for her to take me along."

With her mother's lack of interest in working, Veronica gravitated towards her father's career. Austin's mentorship began when she was young. Growing up, as a way of bonding, the two of them frequently "talked shop" about the goings-on at his office. They read *The Wall Street Journal* together. As an undergraduate in college, Veronica majored in economics and minored in philosophy. She then pursued a master's degree in economics at a prestigious English university. But Sarah was genuinely concerned that these "masculine endeavors" would make it hard for Veronica to attract a husband. Veronica was angry with her mom for making such a "debasing, old-fashioned comment," but the unwelcome idea had inserted itself into her brain. She admits that, to this day, she is reluctant to talk about her work with men she finds romantically appealing.

It's unfortunate that so many of us aren't born with an innate ability not to take things personally. Quite the contrary, when we are hurt by people and situations, it's human nature to feel our own character flaws are the cause. We take hurtful words or deeds at face value. Simultaneously, we're wondering who else can take the blame. Outwardly, Ivy daughters like Veronica, are pointing fingers but internally, they are hurting and blaming themselves. Had she been more self-aware, Veronica might not have ended up on the verge of being fired at work. Sarah wasn't aware how much her actions influenced and would continue to shape Veronica's life decisions past childhood. Sarah clearly was an unhappy woman disappointed about not having a dance career. That her eldest daughter did not (or could not) follow in her footsteps served only as a constant reminder of what Sarah had given up.

25

Unintentionally, Veronica became the personification of Sarah's professional disappointments. As a child, Veronica was unable to grasp the complex feelings that her mother had about being a mom and having a daughter. Veronica only knew that her own needs were not being met. That's why, as an adult, Veronica may have a stronger demand for maternal attention and approval from her female bosses than other women who experienced a different mother-daughter dynamic. Even though she is a grown-up daughter, when Veronica feels ignored, kept out of the loop, or neglected at work, she reacts as if she were still a little girl. The difficult situations at work trigger unconscious feelings from her childhood, and she responds at that level. Veronica's inappropriate behaviors include: giving a coworker the cold shoulder because he was invited to an after-work social function and she wasn't; believing that people are unreasonably "out to get her"; an inability to admit that she could have reacted differently or better in a poor interaction with co-workers; and inappropriately telling colleagues how badly she's been treated. Veronica is still searching for unconditional acceptance and is easily inflamed when the little girl inside of her feels wounded. Like many young children, Veronica the adult is not fully self-aware of her contribution to the negative work environment. Instead of reflecting on her own troublesome actions in the matter, she can only see where others have failed her.

With Ivy daughters, the main problem is that they may not have gotten enough "mothering" from their mothers. It is possible that there might have been some attachment issues at a young age. What Veronica wanted was more of Mom, whether it was emotional support, physical presence, or greater involvement in Veronica's development. Ivy daughters often accumulate a buildup of anger, disappointment, and resentment that they discharge into work settings. They are named after the ivy plant, which can be beautiful and nourishing but can also be poisonous. When allowed to grow unchecked, ivy can spread its clinging vines and choke whatever is in its way. Poison ivy can sneak up on you; you might be itchy one day and the next, have a widespread rash with no idea where it came from. Likewise, Ivy daughters can surprise you with their emotional reactions to things and have no understanding of how harmful or toxic such reactions may be to others.

Before I go further, remember that we're not here to judge our moms' level of involvement with us. Just like your life, your mom's life was (and probably still is) complicated. We cannot possibly understand our mothers' actions or her choices without digging deep into her experiences, as well as into her dynamic with her own mother. One of the most important takeaways from this book is that we should try our very best not to beat ourselves up -- and it's important to do the same for our mothers. Many situations can result in mothers being unable to give their daughters the attention that might have been needed. Some of it comes down to personality, temperament, or fit. Perhaps a mother was not as maternal as her daughter craved; perhaps the daughter needed more attention than what her mother was accustomed to giving because she herself also didn't have a role model for nurturing. In some cases, it might have been that a mother had other demands in her life. If there were other siblings in the house, she couldn't focus all of her time and attention on one child. If money was tight in the household, her first priority was to make sure she could provide for her family, which resulted in her not spending much time with her children because she worked multiple jobs. There are also families where a mother has died, and the daughter is under-parented at an early age. There are mothers who feel that they did everything "right"; they have other daughters who are not Ivy daughters, and they still don't understand how the dynamic with this particular daughter could have been different.

In Veronica's situation, her mother, Sarah, never overcame the trauma of relinquishing her professional ballet dreams. Sarah could only cope by distracting herself with her travel. In more extreme situations, if the daughter was adopted or if her mother was physically or mentally impaired, an Ivy daughter might carry residual abandonment into adulthood. The early years of a daughter's life are crucial in her psychological development, with long lasting effects. Although we are too young to remember much from this time period, we absorb important life lessons that often influence our behavior in adulthood. Even if the dynamic between a mother and her adult daughter changes, that won't fully erase the pattern established between them during the Ivy daughter's preconscious years in childhood.

Some adult Ivy daughters may say they aren't closely connected with their moms, and some may not even have any relationship with them. Others may feel connected but angry with their mothers or still believe they are in competition for her affection or attention. In the office, adult Ivy daughters may seek to fill that void by becoming too involved when managing their employees, as well as having high expectations of support from their supervisors. When things don't go their way at work, their responses to other people seem like an over-reaction. The Ivy daughter wears her neediness on her sleeve and may also express her work dissatisfactions very publicly. When Veronica was issued a disciplinary warning by her manager, her response was to share her negative opinions about a private discussion around the office. She then attempted to reassert her power by forming alliances against her General Manager. If that reminds you of a child having a temper tantrum in the middle of a crowd, you wouldn't be far off base. Veronica's temper tantrums were not as dramatic as a six-year-old's, but they drew a great deal of negative attention. I'll admit that our first few sessions together were tough for both of us. Veronica was resentful initially; one of the first things she said to me was, "I'm sure you're a nice person but this is going to be a waste of time." My attempts to raise her self-awareness were met with defensiveness and an insistence that I didn't fully understand her situation. Rather than getting defensive too, I asked her if she encountered many people who didn't understand her or her situation. She said she was "constantly meeting people who didn't have a clue."

This type of daughter has remarkable energy and is unaware of her own strength. For example, Veronica thought her public joke about her general manager's incompetence was funny, but it wasn't. These daughters may think they are gently brushing up against people, but they actually have thorns which draw blood. They rarely can see how their own actions have contributed to the problems at work; they only see the error of other people's ways. Using the habitual coping behaviors learned in childhood, they react to adult difficulties as children might react, without even being aware of it. Like so many of us, the Ivy daughter places herself in situations that best mimic the environment when she was developing her own preconscious memory. That mimicry includes projecting into the workplace the people and personalities who were part of her early environment. They are like emotional stand-ins who, at least in her mind, replicate the familiar scenarios of her childhood. The sad truth is, this kind of daughter yearns for her needs to be fulfilled but makes that impossible because: (1) she traps herself in a repeating cycle where she is constantly disappointed; and (2) she does not realize that she is putting herself in this self-denying cycle.

How do these daughters perpetuate a self-sabotaging cycle at work? They may choose bosses who don't get involved in the work minutiae (because they are too busy or because it is not his/her work style). Despite any potential dissatisfactions at work, Ivy daughters may have a tendency to stick to their job. If her actions are also causing employer dissatisfaction but the work culture is generally conflict-avoidant, workarounds may evolve around the Ivy daughter (which doesn't help either party but that's a book for another day!) A typical workaround could be the following: She is supposed to generate a report with certain information, and it's clear what that report should include. However, whenever the Ivy daughter runs this report, she never submits it with all of the information. Instead of bringing this to her attention, other employees run their own reports, adding to their workloads, to make sure that the missing information is submitted. Whether she leaves the company or not, an Ivy daughter usually doesn't see how she could have done things better, or differently. Part of the problem may stem from how she communicates. When it comes to receiving bad news, she may have a tendency to fall back on her learned childhood coping mechanisms, which are inappropriate and off-putting. To avoid further conflict, the people around her may avoid telling her that a problem exists. Power may be an especially important value for Ivy daughters -- and why not? Powerful people receive attention and recognition. Psychotherapists have documented over and over, especially in romantic relationships, that while we may believe we are seeking true happiness, what we really seek is familiarity. In our quest for life partners as adults, we are unconsciously trying to recreate the feelings and dynamics we knew in childhood. Think about your past or current adult relationships and how these relationships fulfill your needs. The same is true for work choices. We are trying to satisfy our own wishes, dreams, and aspirations but that often includes repeating dysfunctional dynamics, too.

How does this help? Awareness can set you free. I don't have many Ivy daughter clients. They don't or can't see that they are in part responsible for their workplace challenges. It is important to remember -- and admit -- that there is a bit of the Ivy daughter in every woman. That means each of us will encounter situations that trigger especially sensitive emotions, and it will be hard, if not impossible, for us to avoid responding as an Ivy daughter might. Those who respond predominantly in this manner, like Veronica, usually only meet with me when things have boiled over at the office, inflicting painful problems. In more extreme cases with Ivy daughter clients, I find that there are usually more serious and underlying issues. Recognizing these issues can be a long and hard journey, and the first step is often the most difficult one for an Ivy daughter to take. That involves accepting her own accountability in her workplace woes, which includes admitting that it is not always everyone else's fault. Because the old hurts and the issues lie deep and often involve some type of emotional trauma, I usually recommend psychotherapy with a licensed therapist to my Ivy daughter clients. As in any therapeutic relationship, it should be a professional trusted by the Ivy daughter. This allows her to be both comforted and challenged so that she may begin to understand her past, accept it, and start letting go of the old habits in order to progress. This doesn't happen overnight, but, it's a goal worth pursuing, if you believe that something from your past is interfering with your present work.

I'll never forget the day that Veronica experienced her first breakthrough. I can't claim the credit. Veronica had also started therapy sessions with a psychologist to explore her anger and disappointments in her personal life. We'd been talking about how she felt a keen sense of betrayal and loss when one of her employees, who had been working for Veronica for almost a year, and was her "favorite", announced her resignation. Not only did she handle the news very poorly, she also put her employee in an awkward position when she asked tearfully, "How could you do this to me?" The employee was leaving to do something more creative. Veronica commented to me that she had no interest in artistic endeavors. She was already transitioning to another subject when she stopped herself, looked me in the eyes and said, "Say, you don't think this has something to do with Mama, do you? When she was home, Mama was always too busy with her artsy things to have much to do with me." I wanted to leap out of my seat and throw my hands in the air! On that day, Veronica opened a window into her inner self, something that she had never done before.

There is hope for Ivy daughters. There always is hope. If you believe you are one, remember that we are gifted with tens of thousands of days, and each new one is an opportunity for us to say to ourselves: "Today, I'm going to do better. I'm going to be better. Yesterday is over. Today, I'm going to do my best to be my best." Don't lose faith in yourself. Don't believe you are alone in this, even though the first step often requires you (and you alone) to have the courage to ask for help from others. What might surprise you is that when you do, people will step up. Ivy daughters have the ability to move beyond their workplace challenges. They can become calmer, more self-aware women who understand the triggers to their behaviors. They can learn how to make informed decisions that lead them away from the old cycle of disappointments.

Conclusion

It might be enough to recognize yourself as an Ivy daughter. That's okay. It's also okay if you don't believe that you fit neatly into one category. My daughtering model is designed to show how women can get stuck or can be catapulted based on their relationships with their moms. It's not meant to over-categorize, pigeonhole or label. Representing the youngest, the Ivy daughter needs the most care and attention. But note that she isn't necessarily separate and distinct from the other daughters. Regardless of the type of relationship we may have had with our moms, there's an Ivy daughter in all of us. After all, none of us had all of our needs met in infancy and early childhood. There IS no such thing as a perfect mother. As I mentioned in the introduction, even the mother who meets every one of her child's needs does not end up with a perfect relationship. All people grow by being out of their comfort zone. Needing to step up and feed yourself, dress yourself, and take care of others is important in developing into a self-sufficient woman. Just wait until you read more about Bootstrap daughters, and this will become obvious.

If you think you might be an Ivy daughter and are wondering what's next, here are some tips that will help you move forward the next time something goes wrong at work. These tips are useful if you've yet to find your ideal career or if you are considering a career change. We all must accept what we have and how we came to be who we are. For Ivy daughters, this may feel daunting. Their challenges may include learning to let go of the anger and disappointment. In some households, other family members may have stepped in to care for Ivy daughters if their moms could not provide the care needed. That's the amazing thing about people -- two women with the same mother can, and often do, develop differently. While the Ivy daughter got lost in her mother's unavailability, her sister could have assumed the role of primary caregiver, becoming a Bootstrap daughter. Just because you're an Ivy daughter doesn't mean you'll always be one. When Ivy daughters are placed in situations where they are needed, many find themselves responding well to the new and unfamiliar challenges. This can happen when Ivy daughters start their own families, especially around the presence of children. They often realize that their own past hurts or unfulfilled needs don't matter so much anymore – they're outweighed by the need to provide the best future for the entire family. Caring for elderly, infirm parents can also have this effect. The Ivy daughter might even, at some point, begin to understand that her mother did the best she could and might not have been mothered well herself.

Ivy daughters can grow up to become calm and confident women, but they can only do so when they move past this stage.

Tip #1: Stop the Blame Game: Examine your patterns!

As a counselor, I often help clients look at patterns of problems. These patterns offer more information than individual situations. Ivy daughters might wonder why problems follow them to work. A few self-aware daughters have asked me, "Am I creating this drama?" The point is, whether a woman is creating it or unconsciously choosing situations that may repeat old dysfunctional relationships (or some combination of the two), the first step is to make the unconscious more conscious. Ivy daughters should take stock of themselves and their situations when they encounter something that isn't working for them. For example, when a woman finds herself frustrated or upset with the people in the office around her, she should ask herself what she's bringing to the situation and think about whether the problems she's currently facing are similar to previous ones. She should consider what she (not anyone else) can do to change the results the next time. When she applies this simple awareness, self-reflection and accountability, she takes a huge leap forward to solving her own problems.

Tip #2: Watch and Learn

People let others know how they want to be treated. Ivy daughters are encouraged to watch others, and take their cues from the people they like to be around and whom they respect. How are they treating others? Remember that the best form of flattery is imitation.

Tip #3: It's Not All About You!

I tell my clients who are Ivy daughters to try their best to let go of the minor hang-ups at work. I ask, "Would you rather argue about how a sentence is phrased in a report, or have people listen to you when the numbers for a major account are off?" No matter how competent an Ivy daughter is, if she has a reputation for being "difficult" at work, it will compromise the respect she ultimately wishes to receive.

Tip #4: Be a Superhero and Use Your Power for Good

If an Ivy daughter is in a leadership position, she needs to be careful not to take advantage of it. Being a leader is a delicate balancing act. If a manager constantly sends instant messages like, "See me please", she may not realize that it makes people want to avoid her. Whenever possible, hold face-to-face conversations and always follow the Golden Rule: "Do unto others as you would have done to yourself." If an Ivy daughter is not sure how to better manage her employees, she should seek help. Help doesn't always have to come in the form of a career coach or counselor; it can be enrolling in a management course or pairing up with a mentor.

Tip #5: If You Wear It, They Will Come

When a person takes the time to "wear someone else's shoes," as the old adage advises -- for a week, a day, or even a moment -- she will find herself empathizing with others

34

more. Ivy daughters should ask questions gently, and listen carefully to the answers.

Tip #6: Ask for a 360-degree Feedback at Work

Most Ivy daughters are in the dark about their impact on others. It's extremely useful to have the opportunity to check on whether your beliefs are grounded in reality. In a 360-degree feedback, a person is evaluated by his or her colleagues, clients, managers, and any other person with whom she interacts. Though this might feel threatening, it can yield invaluable information when administered correctly by a coach or HR professional. Often, 360-degree feedbacks reveal distinct patterns of behavior which can be enormously helpful to this kind of daughter, fostering greater clarity about how the pain of her relationship with her mom may be carried into the workplace.

Tip #7: Pour the Unmet Needs into a Good Cause

Ivy daughters are passionate! When this energy is appropriately channeled, the sky's the limit. Amazing things can and do happen. Ivy daughters are capable of being great advocates for the underdogs, and they also may excel when faced with other worthy challenges. If we examine the causes in which people choose to invest their time, money, and energy, often the cause is somehow related to a personal situation or trauma. This is a great way to work through unfinished business between Ivy daughters and their mothers.

Tip #8: Be Accountable for Another Life

Taking care of another life could mean adopting a puppy, kitten, iguana, or goldfish. The point is, that Ivy daughters do well when someone or something else needs their care and attention. The result is that Ivy daughters may develop a more nurturing and mature approach to life.

Chapter 3:

The Maverick Daughter

When Gillian came to me about her workplace woes, she wasn't looking for a career change. She was looking for a drama-free place to work. Gillian admitted that she didn't feel like she had a career; instead, she'd held a series of jobs, as a career was "too big of a nut to crack". She found the prospect of thinking beyond her immediate issue overwhelming. So we focused on the matter at hand, her most recent job at a call center. "Carmen is my battle axe of a boss," she said. "She had the nerve to tell me, in front of everybody, that I show up late to work. Can you imagine?" In Gillian's mind, the company didn't pay her enough to put up with "rude callers and demanding bosses." She'd somehow drawn the short end of the stick when it came to workplaces. "Everyone was so catty," she reflected. Sometimes Gillian wondered if things might have been different, if she hadn't dropped out of college, if she hadn't spent that year backpacking across Europe, if she had taken that job offer in Los Angeles more seriously.

Throughout the years, she zigged and zagged from one job to another -- whatever came along to pay the bills. She'd been the receptionist at a lumberyard, she had worked a few, disastrous months in Paris as an au pair, she'd waitressed. When she married Joe, a bartender in Pasadena, she thought it was time to find a "real" job, but she didn't have any idea what she wanted to do or how to find this out. Prior to her call center job, she'd worked as an administrative assistant at four companies in three years. She admitted to me that she hated working in an office and believed the work was beneath her. She didn't respect Carmen, her boss at the call center, and her previous bosses hadn't fared any better.

A Maverick daughter's behavior can be remarkably changeable. They want to closely connect with their moms in one moment; but, abruptly and without explanation, they retreat to be on their own. The word maverick is defined in the dictionary as non-conformist, free spirit, or unorthodox. Many women who are Maverick daughters would also describe themselves similarly. See if the following statements sound familiar: You don't necessarily do what you're told and when you do, it's on your terms; you're an explorer, so the idea of starting over excites you; you like to chase new opportunities; when you really want something or someone, you go after it with astonishing focus and drive.

What most of these daughters have in common is the adolescent relationship they continue to have with their moms in adulthood. Their mothers like to give a lot of direction, advice, or opinions about their adult children's choices. Maverick daughters tend to react negatively to their mothers' attempts to become over-involved in their lives. The daughters reject this and want more independence. After most conversations with her mother, Gillian, for example, will inevitably receive a text asking what's wrong. "Most of the time, she wants to know why I've abruptly ended a perfectly good chat with her. I don't know what she's talking about; I just had other things to do." While her mother's questions may have baffled Gillian, deep down she couldn't disagree that there was some merit to what her mother pointed out. She often feels thoroughly annoyed when talking to her mother. The only problem was that Gillian couldn't quite put her finger on the underlying issues.

Many women might have been through some version of Gillian's experience. They may sympathize with her not only because they have similar interactions with their mothers, but also because they may be a little lost professionally and may have a hard time with authority.

However, if this happens on a regular basis, it could have nothing to do with simple chance or bad luck. Some women may have the self-awareness to wonder why they're consistently unhappy at work. These daughters, however, remain unaware that they are not aligning their jobs with their interests, skills, values, and personality. When there is a misalignment, there is less potential for success or happiness. Many of these daughters do not have fully formed career identities. The job choices they make are based on convenience, often stumbled into by circumstances, and with little connection to the women's identities or ambitions. So, not surprisingly, these daughters are dissatisfied at work.

Throughout the childhood years, many Maverick daughters describe their moms as being "involved", but not in a comfortable way. It's not unusual for a mom to love her "precious, little girl" or to identify with her or to fantasize that her daughter will be just like her, but Maverick daughters tell me that their moms lavished a little too much attention on them. As babies, we need constant attention. But as we grow older, we become more independent and want to explore the world around us -- sometimes with Mom, but growing girls also desire to do this by themselves. Separation is a natural process. Adolescent girls need to discover who they are, independent from their mothers, which includes discovering their own interests, style of dress, and choice of friends. It's also perfectly natural for mothers to feel hurt and even a little betrayed when their daughters decide to do things on their own or move in different directions. Plenty of mothers want their little girls to remain their little girls forever, at least in many ways. They want their daughters to always turn to them for help and perhaps even be their friends.

A mother may also live vicariously through her daughter. Without realizing it, she could believe doing so is a way to resolve her own childhood wounds and issues, especially if she did not have the same opportunities as her daughter. If you're feeling quick to judge Mom's actions, don't. Unless a child is subjected to extreme situations like abuse or neglect, there are no right and wrong methods of motherhood. Mothers are also unique and have their own mothering needs. Sometimes these needs conflict with their daughters' needs.

Mothers of Maverick daughters tend to hold on tightly to their children instead of letting go. They are vigilant parents, whether it's due to love, fear, envy, empathy, or any other reason. They may believe that is how they should be, or they may have trouble letting go because the attachment is so deep. Their daughters, however, might feel like an ant under a magnifying glass with the hot sun shining directly overhead. Even when a mom's intent is good, it can be an uncomfortable situation over a prolonged period. Every girl (and boy) has to go through a healthy separation to fully become themselves. These daughters squirm under the scrutiny and react by pulling away, physically or mentally. Some daughters move halfway across the country to try to establish an emotional separation. But even that may not work. At some point, we all desire to be independent. It usually happens during our teenage years, which are famous for inflicting some of the toughest growing pains on both parents and children. Think about typical teenage acts of rebellion: defying rules; acting out; deliberately doing the opposite of what was asked. It doesn't have to be overt, grand gestures. Sometimes it can even be that time you snapped at Mom when she reminded you to wear a sweater before going out. These daughters tend to initiate many adolescent pushbacks, well past their teenage years, and with anyone they might unconsciously view as a maternal or authority figure. Though they are now adults, they are still struggling to gain control.

Remember, we don't come with instruction manuals, and this book is not a time machine. My goal is not to go into all of the "coulda/woulda/shouldas" of how a mother dealt with her separation from her daughter. My goal is twofold: (1) to bring more awareness to adult daughters of the connection between what they learned when they were children and how it might be driving their reactions in the workplace; and (2) to give adult daughters the tools they need to move beyond reactions and go forward in their careers.

My first sessions with Gillian delved into her family history and in particular, her relationship with her mother, Helen. Helen was a source of embarrassment for her. "She treated my friends like they were *her* friends -- if they came over for a sleepover, she'd want to be in on all the girl talk. And the way she dressed? She was constantly 'borrowing' my clothes. It drove me crazy. She always had to be the center of attention." Throughout her childhood, Helen was eager for Gillian to come home immediately after school. She would "grill" Gillian about what was going on with her friends and loved hearing gossip and rumors. Gillian said that whenever she tried to tell her mom she didn't want to do what Helen wanted at the exact moment Helen wanted it done, her mother would get unreasonably upset with her. Sometimes she would accuse Gillian of not loving her enough.

During Gillian's teenage years, Helen became increasingly more critical. She didn't like Gillian's new friends because she thought they were a bad influence. When Gillian had her nose pierced, Helen's only comment was, "Great, now you've been branded like a cow." She also criticized Gillian for purposely failing to apply herself in her studies. Gillian and Helen would go through periods of "stonewalled silence" or end up in "screaming matches." One week after finishing high school, Gillian packed up her meager belongings and moved out of the house.

It's not all bad. As Gillian and I continued to work on her career issues, she shared with me many moments of Helen being incredibly supportive. Gillian felt guilty each time she shared negative aspects of her mother with me and wanted me to know about the positive ones as well. The relationship between a mother and her daughter is intense and delicate. It may leave both mother and daughter extremely critical of one another, but at the same time concerned about, and protective of, one another. Gillian's mother was a talented seamstress and made the most creative, custom costumes for school plays every year. Gillian could ask Helen direct questions about anything and trust that the truth was being spoken in response. If Gillian was in trouble, Helen would be ready to help her through it, no matter if they had just gotten into one of their epic fights. Gillian wanted closeness with Helen, the way that she noticed other daughters seemed to naturally have with their moms. She confessed to me that she "wanted to want to" call Helen every day, but she couldn't make herself do it. "I think about picking up the phone, just to say hello, how are you doing, whatever. But then I know that it's not going to be a simple conversation. She'll want to know every little detail in my life. Then that will somehow end up with questions about what's going on with Joe. Why aren't we having kids already? Why can't I stay at the same company for more than a year?" Helen had many ideas about what Gillian should do for a living and was not shy about sharing them. "Everything snowballs into one big 'I told you so.' Like it always does. I can only deal with Mom in small doses -- with a lot of space in between."

The Maverick daughter feels compelled to do the opposite of what her mom says and does. Although her parents both went to college, Gillian dropped out after a semester. She didn't see the point and she didn't want to "be like her mother." There's a little bit of this daughter in all of us -- my mother was a psychoanalyst, and when I was choosing a major, I remember specifically not wanting to pursue social work/psychology because I always thought of it as my "Mom's thing." I was absolutely certain that the entire field of psychology could not possibly allow for Mom and me to have separate, specialized careers. Here's the catch, though: when women make decisions not to be like their mothers without considering their own interests and goals, they could end up on the wrong path. That's the underlying issue for these daughters, the nub that they can't seem to grasp through all of the job-hopping, the difficult bosses, and the toxic feelings about work in general. At the heart of the matter, these daughters are confused about who they are and what they want to do. If the only thing a woman knows is that she may want to do the opposite of her mother (or any authority figure who follows), despite all of her accomplishments and adventures, an adult daughter has limited herself. By closing herself off in this manner, she becomes inflexible about what could lead her towards a happier, more fulfilling professional life. How can we truly know what we want or don't want if we base it on what someone else wants or doesn't want?

When I pointed this out to Gillian, she physically recoiled from me. She couldn't, or wouldn't, see what was chasing her and what she was running away from all these years. I went through the situations in her work life that made Gillian a classic Maverick daughter: how she tended to describe her female bosses as "nagging"; how she spent years job-hopping and how her previous vocations were wildly different from one another; how she kept ending up in workplaces where the office politics made work an uncomfortable or anxiety-inducing event. I pointed out that much of this came from Gillian, unconsciously, recreating her dynamic with her mother, Helen, from all those years ago. Helen was a little too overpowering for Gillian's personality, and she reacted by defying Helen, actually doing the opposite of what she advised. Now, Gillian works for bosses who are too demanding or tend to micromanage Gillian's work. Since she doesn't have a college degree, she has closed herself off to the job opportunities that might have provided a more enriching work experience. By reflexively doing the opposite of her mother, Gillian never learned how to develop a career strategy.

By now, I hope it's clear that Gillian's mother had great influence on her. That is the case for all daughters, whether you are a Maverick or not. So, what's Mom still got to do with how Maverick daughters go about their professional lives today? Gillian thought that putting physical distance between herself and her mom would solve the problem. She thought that a literal escape would set her free. Maybe it did, for a little while. But she didn't account for the old feelings pushed deep down inside that grew and festered. These old feelings are automatic emotional responses set up to deal with a mom who needed a little too much attention from her daughter. They don't go away just because a woman is not physically near the source that created them anymore. Think of these old automatic responses as hidden landmines. Step on a trigger, and it sets off a reaction. It is an unfortunate Catch-22 for Maverick daughters; they want to avoid stepping on these emotional landmines even as they helplessly, and unconsciously, gravitate towards them. Without being aware of what makes her tick and what triggers those landmines, a Maverick daughter will continue to repeat the pattern of working in a job or company that makes her feel trapped. In turn, this trapped feeling compels women to free themselves, often through subtle and direct forms of rebellion. Rebellion doesn't just have to be about quitting outright or bouncing from one job to the next. It can be any of the following: deliberately leaving a work assignment incomplete; challenging authority; glossing over the important details of an assignment because she believes she already knows the best way to do the work. In this way, rather than moving beyond the adolescent stage of their lives, Maverick daughters are prolonging it -- sometimes by years, sometimes by decades, sometimes indefinitely.

Conclusion

Does the prospect of being a perpetual teenager fill you with dread? If you said "yes," then I'm here to tell you that you don't have to face that prospect, if you don't want to. You have the power to leap forward. At the end of this chapter, I have some tips that you can start using right away. In Chapter 9, I expand on these and offer additional resources that can help you climb out of your unhappiness and dissatisfaction at work. When Maverick daughters realize the kind of work that makes them passionate, watch out! Once their potential is unleashed and realized, they can take whichever profession they choose by storm and break all kinds of barriers. That's the great thing about Maverick daughters -- what was once considered performance flaws that held them back can be repurposed to propel them forward. This also changes the dynamic for future generations of women. A daughter of this type who is self-aware is more likely to have the kind of relationship with her own children that she yearned to have with her mother, a healthy and intimate connection that allows the future generation of daughters to separate with less pain and drama. Self-aware daughters are more likely to realize holding on too tightly only encourages their daughters to push away harder. So the new generation of daughters raised by these moms will be able to better recognize, follow, and be inspired by their mothers' accomplishments.

As for Gillian, before our sessions stalled, she had started to consider the possibility of going back to school. But that was put on hold indefinitely while she went through divorce proceedings. After the divorce was finalized, she moved to a new city in a new state for a fresh start. These days she's working as a personal shopper at a high end clothing retail shop. She thinks this job is better than the call center, but she's still dissatisfied and wondering about her next steps. Gillian is a bright woman with so much potential and so much to offer. I hope, when she's ready again, that we can resume our sessions.

If you're living in a similar adolescent, rebellious state in your career or work relationships, it's time to assert your independence in a healthier way! I understand and empathize with your desire and need to do your own thing, but it's okay to stop fighting authority, be it your mom or society itself. Here are some tips to start changing the dynamic. When the persistent problems are no longer perpetuated, women can begin to find their true professional selves.

Tip #:1 Change "I Should" to "I Want"

When we find ourselves avoiding healthy changes in our lives, sometimes it's because we feel like we *should* stop doing something. This can very well be leftover pressure from when we were told what we should and should not do. Logic and human behavior don't always follow the same path. We know that imposing tight restrictions on ourselves generally only makes things worse and, in the end, can lead to the exact opposite. Did you ever feel like you should stay late to finish a project? If it happens often, that might make you resent your boss, and could cause you to look for a new job. However, try changing how you think about staying late. Decide that you're staying late because you want to, since it potentially means less work the next day. You may find less negativity and provocation because you've chosen to willingly stay. Converting SHOULD to WANT helps release you from the continued adolescent battle with your your mom.

Tip #2: Find new ways to communicate at work.

Two extreme reactions that Maverick daughters may have learned from their childhood is either to lash out or to avoid their mothers. This manifests itself at work when, after an argument, adult Maverick daughters slam doors or loudly retreat to their offices to show their frustrations. These reactions aren't healthy but, because they're familiar ones, they resurface more dramatically in the workplace for Maverick daughters. This reaction is something one would expect from an adolescent. Maverick daughters may fall back on these patterns, especially when feeling extreme emotions like anger. Instead of lashing out or keeping these emotions repressed, though, try to express your thoughts directly. This may involve attending workshops on assertiveness training for women. These workshops are not about acting aggressively; they teach people how to be direct and clear without apologies or hostility. Learning how to communicate at work in the face of uncomfortable situations can be very challenging for Maverick daughters, but with a commitment to doing so, practice, and hard work, adult daughters can learn to manage their emotions and find healthier ways of resolving conflict.

Tip #3: Check the Impulse

Sometimes, when we rebel against authority, it is to assert our independence. What we don't realize, though, is that we end up hurting ourselves in the process. Maverick daughters may be impulsive. They generally live in the moment, which could mean some clearly self-destructive practices: abrupt changes in jobs based on their current interests or whims; showing up for work at their discretion, regardless of any explicitly communicated work schedule; and, acting contrary about small matters just for the sake of being "right." My advice to Maverick daughters is to get out of the moment, or take a moment before giving in to their career impulses. I tell them to think about why they're compelled to move in one direction over another in their career choices. Were they able to go through a healthy separation process with their mothers? Thinking about the mother-daughter dynamic may allow Maverick daughters to better understand their impulsivity, and to distinguish the differences between a maternal figure and an authority figure at work. When Maverick daughters can start to make choices for themselves for reasons other than a prolonged teenage rebellion, then they have worked through a major obstacle.

Tip #4: Career Thoughtfulness

Maverick daughters cannot establish roots in any one career because their choices are not grounded in self-assessment. For that to occur, one must look inside oneself to assess true interests, skills, values and personality in order to make decisions based on these critical elements. In Chapter 9, I provide more details about career thoughtfulness, along with useful tips and solutions.

Tip #5: Be the Grown Up

The best words I can give to Maverick daughters is that they are no longer being controlled. Nobody -- not their mother, their boss, or anyone else -- has power over them. Whether it's growing up or dealing with a micromanaging boss, there is no longer a need to resist. A grown woman has choices. She has the authority to make substantive changes in her life instead of recreating old and familiar patterns. She has the power to make her own choices. She can start making decisions as the grownup that she really is.

Chapter 4:

The Butterfly Daughter

When Sofia was six months old, her parents divorced and her father moved across the country for a job opportunity. To make ends meet, her mother, Andrea, worked three part-time jobs. Fortunately, they lived with Sofia's grandparents (Andrea's parents), so there were almost always adults around to take care of Sofia while her mother worked. Andrea always encouraged Sofia to focus on doing well in school and pursuing her dreams. Sofia explained, "Mom married young, because of me. She didn't even finish high school. She told me the minute I was born, nothing else mattered as much as I did. But she wanted to make sure that whatever choices I ended up making, I would be better prepared for the difficulties in life than she had been."

Sofia heeded her mother's advice carefully. "Mom was so proud of me the day I received my high school diploma. She took the whole day off from work, which was almost unheard of! But that wasn't the best part. The best part was that Mom watching me walk across the stage in my cap and gown gave her the impetus to go back to school." While Andrea added night school GED courses to her already busy schedule, Sofia studied graphic design in college. Andrea had encouraged Sofia to explore her talents and when it became apparent that she favored art above all else, Andrea scraped up the resources for trips to museums, extracurricular lessons, and other enriching endeavors. In turn, Sofia decided she wanted a career that had both a creative component and financial stability. Graphic design was the best of both worlds, and it was work that she truly enjoyed. After college, she found an entry-level job at a design firm which allowed her to gain significant experience in the field. Today, she has a successful small business of her own and her work has been featured both nationally and internationally.

Andrea was not a conventional role model for Sofia's professional goals. She was, in many ways, a guide for Sofia on what not to do career-wise. Yet unlike Maverick daughters, Sofia did not reject all of her mother's actions or advice. Andrea was not overly controlling and supported her daughter's interests and dreams, however different they were from her own. As a mother, Andrea did not make Sofia's childhood about herself. Sofia could separate from her mother with less difficulty than other daughters in this book. She was able to select the lessons from her mother's life that would serve her well in the workplace: namely, to persevere, to have patience, and to be accountable. But to fill in any blanks that her mother could not provide as a role model for guiding her through career challenges, Sofia learned to trust her instincts. At times, that also meant asking for help from peers and more experienced designers. Fortunately, she had excellent interpersonal relationships; managers and colleagues said she worked well within teams, while clients were happy with her deliverables. In this way, people naturally gravitated to her. Leaders recognized her talents and presented her with opportunities for mentorship. These mentors became the career role models that Sofia's mother could not be for her.

By now, maybe you've read the other chapters and thought to yourself, "I might have been a little bit of an Ivy or Maverick daughter a long time ago, but I'm not anymore." Or, after reading ahead, you may empathize with the Copycat or Bootstrap daughter, but you don't strongly identify with them either. When I first created this model, I had in mind the Ivy, Maverick, Copycat, and Bootstrap daughters. But as time passed, it became apparent that the model was incomplete. Missing here were all the women who had relationships with emotionally available mothers who could not be role models for their careers.

Elton John's song "Someone Saved My Life Tonight" comes to mind when I think about the Butterfly daughter, especially the lyrics:

You're a butterfly
And butterflies are free to fly
Fly away, high away, bye bye

Though the topic of the song is about something unrelated, the above lyrics describe Butterfly daughters perfectly. They were free to fly because their mothers (and fathers) allowed it. They flew away from their family of origin and the patterns that were set for them. A Butterfly daughter went through a beautiful metamorphosis with support from her mother and other members of her family. Even if her mother was unable to realize her own career potential, she encouraged her Butterfly daughter to be her best. Many Butterfly daughters are successful, professional, and independent women. But this scenario isn't perfect (as there are no perfect scenarios). A Butterfly daughter may feel more connected with her father or other family members because they were the Butterfly daughter's role models for her career. Even as close as she may be with her mother, a Butterfly daughter may believe there's something missing in the mother-daughter dynamic. To a certain degree, these daughters understand that they are supposed to "be like" their mothers. However, due to the differences in their careers and lifestyle, a Butterfly daughter may not be able to relate to her own mother, and vice versa. She may struggle to understand some of her choices. To the undiscerning eye, the Butterfly daughter is successful (maybe even privileged), but she struggles internally with bouts of lacking confidence and feelings of self-doubt. She might wonder why men from similar backgrounds appear more self-assured.

Butterfly daughters may be the first women in their families to go to college or to have a successful profession.

While it may appear that, like Maverick daughters, they chose a career path that is opposite or very different from their mothers, Butterfly daughters differ from Maverick daughters because they do not rebel against their mothers' advice or decisions for the sake of rebellion. Instead, they are making informed decisions with their mothers' support and guidance. Sofia's mother, Andrea, did not have the same opportunities as her daughter in the workplace. Andrea wanted to make sure that Sofia made the most of opportunities to create a better life for herself and future generations. Andrea and other mothers of Butterfly daughters wanted something different for their daughters. Many of them saw that the opportunities for women were changing and expanding. They raised their daughters without pushing too hard one way or the other. The daughters were then free to explore their own interests.

Regardless of status, Butterfly daughters find their own way. I want to share Rita's story with you as well. Rita's childhood was very different from Sofia's, but that doesn't make her any less of a Butterfly daughter. Rita's parents (father Peter and mother Camille) were happily married and both educated professionals. Their decision to have children -- Rita was the youngest -- had been extensively planned and carefully executed. When Camille became a mother, she scaled back from her full-time job and worked 25 hours per week instead. Living in a Texan suburb, Rita's earliest memories are of her mother and father taking their family to a baseball game. Peter and Camille enjoyed a healthy and fit lifestyle, which they encouraged as much as possible in all of their children. They all participated in different sports; for Rita, it was soccer and swimming. Rita was an avid reader and often curled up on a Saturday afternoon with her nose buried into a book. "That used to drive my mom crazy," Rita says with a rueful laugh. "She said she didn't understand how I could sit all those hours at school reading and then come home to do it some more. Mom was always really critical about the state of physical education at school, so she was always pushing us to keep our bodies fit. Junk food was a big no-no in the house."

As the years went by, Rita's parents placed more and more emphasis on physical health. When it became clear that she was an unusually fast swimmer, her parents discussed hiring a coach with the ultimate goal of Rita competing professionally. Before any of this could come to fruition, however, Rita was hurt in an accident. While not life-threatening, it did end any hopes of her becoming a professional swimmer. She remembers it as "one of the best summers ever" because she was finally able to read all the books she wanted without her mom saying a word. "We lived in a small town where football and baseball were the primary sources of entertainment on a Friday night. My dad studied sports medicine, and my mom was the assistant cheerleading coach at school. They always found time to shuttle us to our junior league games and never said no if we wanted to go to hockey or basketball or lacrosse camp. But debate club? Chorus? Those were hobbies we could enjoy if we had time in between games and practice."

Rita was somewhat at a loss when she enrolled in college. Camille suggested physical therapy, which Rita took up. It was an interesting profession, and Rita didn't mind it. During the six years that followed, Rita graduated, became involved in a very committed relationship, and started working. The day that changed Rita's perspective was when she showed Camille a house that she was thinking of buying with her boyfriend. Camille liked the house very much and recommended that Rita hire a contractor to build a private office on the first floor. "Mom told me that once I got married and started having kids, working from home part-time would be a great way to go." Rita experienced a flash of what her future would be like, how eerily it resembled Camille's, a part-time working mom advocating physical fitness. Because she'd seen what it was like for her mom, she knew how it would be for herself and wasn't sure she wanted the same thing right away. She wondered if her mother might have felt the same way too, once upon a time. Rita made the decision to see what else was out there. She quit her job and gave into a secret desire she'd never told her mom about. She moved to New York City. "It was crazy because the only thing I knew about New York City was what I'd seen on TV and movies. But I wanted to experience something high-energy and completely different from home. I thought, what could be more different than the Big Apple?"

Besides uprooting herself to a new and unfamiliar city, Rita changed her career track as well. She had many fond memories cooking with her mother, particularly taking recipes and making healthier versions of them. The "no junk food" rule strictly enforced during childhood had stuck with Rita. She went back to school, became a nutritionist and started a food blog. Rita was surprised at the night-and-day difference in her level of satisfaction about work; it changed from being "just okay" to something she looked forward to doing every day. Her mother Camille's initial response was concern. Would she be able to relate to Rita's new experiences? If she couldn't, then Camille couldn't help her daughter anymore. At the same time, Camille respected and admired the courage that Rita displayed in pursuing these goals.

Within the last century, the expectations visualized for a woman's place in society have opened up far beyond hearth and home. Today, we don't have to be defined solely as wife and mother, unless we choose to define ourselves this way. Many of us also choose to work outside of the home and, when possible, to take on senior positions at companies. Rita chose to go one step further. Camille had an established career and family life. Rita could have followed in Camille's footsteps and done well, but instead Rita tried something different. After thinking about what she really wanted, she decided to strike out entirely on her own. Doing so, Rita took a big risk; she knew she would have to face challenges and major decisions without the practical guidance her mother had previously been able to give her.

Even with all of the wonderful advancements spurred by the women's liberation movement, leadership positions in many businesses are still predominantly held by men. Though that is slowly changing, there is a noticeable gap between today's women and their mothers, grandmothers, and great-grandmothers. That's why role models are so important for women in the workforce now. The skills needed to succeed at work are still a mystery for many of us. Women don't have the same advantages that help men succeed in the workplace, namely generations of career role models. There is no such historical guidance yet for women. If their mothers are not able to provide them with this instruction, then the daughters must learn to do it on their own. Butterfly daughters are paving the way for the first time. You cannot underestimate the internal gaps of doubt created in women who didn't have moms as a role model for career.

There is a common theme among Butterfly daughters: those who are struggling with some aspect of their career might be holding on to a sense of what their mothers did or did not accomplish. A commonly asked question from Butterfly daughters is, "If my mother couldn't do this, why do I think I can?" Another is, "I couldn't possibly be smarter than my parents. Could I?" My response to them is, why not? Do we question why we're taller than our parents? Why can't we imagine that we could surpass them professionally? Butterfly daughters have the drive and ambition to succeed, even without a role model, but they may have repressed uncertainties about whether they are doing their job "correctly." This stems from the lack of guidance their mothers could give because they did not perform work at a comparable level. Since the Butterfly daughter had to figure it out on her own, she may view each challenge in her path as one with a steep learning curve (even if she has faced previous similar obstacles before). Butterfly daughters often don't realize their own worth. If the grownups in her childhood worked unsatisfying but stable jobs, she may alternatively choose to pursue a profession that would fulfill her dreams.

So many Butterfly daughters regret making some decisions without a career role model. Many told me that if they'd had a role model, those choices would have been very different. Despite their successes, many Butterfly daughters felt they weren't smart enough to get a Ph.D., while others acknowledged that they were actually creating their own glass ceilings. Still others didn't know what to do at certain career junctions. Most common of all is Butterfly daughters believing they are "frauds" and imposters in their work roles. They feel like what they've achieved in the workplace is somehow undeserved. They also fear that people will discover they don't really know what they are talking about.

Research shows that many women who have high skills for STEM careers (in science, technology, engineering and mathematics) hesitate to move in that direction. The lack of interest may be due to fear of entering a "man's" world but also could be because there are still so few women role models in these areas.

If a Butterfly daughter's mother stayed home, she may feel conflicted, if she chooses not to do the same with her own children. Most women face extremely complicated decisions on whether or not to have children, and whether or not to work while raising them. Women's choices in this area may be driven by financial need because of the expenses associated these days with having children. It is difficult for many families to survive without two incomes, and in single-parent households, the mothers typically must also work. When women, particularly Butterfly daughters, have the financial means to stay home and their mothers stayed home, they may feel great guilt about working. Many Butterfly daughters tend to be aware and appreciative of the nurturing they received from their own mothers; they want to "pay it forward" and provide the same to their own kids. She may feel this is more important than pursuing a career after her children are born. A Butterfly daughter who makes this decision may believe her decision to stay at home benefits her own daughter in many ways, but the disadvantage is, she won't be able to serve as a role model when it comes to her daughter's career choices. Whether or not she chooses employment, the Butterfly daughter may feel a certain isolation (even with a supporting, loving family around her) for walking a different route than her mom. Or, she may feel guilt at surpassing her mother's financial, professional, or social status.

Once they make a decision about the profession that they want to pursue, Butterfly daughters generally tend to stick with it. While many build successes on their chosen path, others may be underemployed, or believe that they are not being compensated for their full worth. Though they have these aggravations, they may not know how to properly open up these subjects, or, because they have invested so much in their job, they may not know how to walk away. As a result, Butterfly daughters may find it hard to enter and stay on a leadership track. They might think they are limited to being Number Two, never Number One.

Because of the careful thought and big investment behind their career decisions, Butterfly daughters are more risk averse than many other women and avoid diverging from their career paths. When transitions are imposed on them, it can throw them for a loop. They may find themselves lost when that happens. Being laid off or fired from a job may be extremely unsettling or stressful for these women because they strongly identify with their work. When that has been taken away involuntarily, they may perceive a large portion of their identity being stripped as well. Should their unemployment extend for a longer duration than they anticipate, depression can set in. This daughter is often held up as an exemplary model for other family members and, if she's out of work, the entire family may be anxious about her state. It is both a comfort and a burden for the Butterfly daughter.

Conclusion

Butterfly daughters have the drive and the ambition, thanks in part to their mothers allowing them to pursue different goals. But without role models, they may face more obstacles in meeting those goals. However, they are passionate about their line of work. Thanks to the healthy support and separation from their mothers, they should be aware that this gives them a powerful advantage not only in their professional outlook but in life in general. They have the ability to explore their interests and to make informed decisions about those interests. They are not afraid to follow or to stray from their mothers' footsteps, even if doing so may bring on uncertainty, doubt, and insecurity. When this happens, I tell them that it's okay and I remind them of their accomplishments so far. They have more potential to unlock, and there will always be some risk in unlocking it. Everyone must leave their comfort zone to grow, regardless of the daughter type they most resemble. Luckily for the Butterfly daughter, her ability to do so is not hampered by an out-of-balance mother-daughter dynamic. It's one of the reasons why she can more easily see that the sky's the limit when pursuing her career ambitions.

Tip #1: Identify the Fear

We often avoid doing things because we fear them. However, fear is an illusion of "false expectations appearing real." In its path, many people are immobilized. For Butterfly daughters facing this dilemma, I encourage them to step back from their situations and identify the fear by putting a name to it. For example, even though she wants to further develop her career, Jane is reluctant to transfer to a new company with better opportunities. A reason she gives me is that she "likes her colleagues too much." What's really going on here is that Jane is afraid of the changes that come with a new job -- she might not get along as well with the people there, so she might not be as effective. When a person understands the underlying fear in the matter, they increase their chances of dealing with it and determining whether these concerns have merit. In Jane's case, she reminded herself of her proven track record as a skilled and valued employee in all her jobs. She concluded that her fear was not insurmountable, and she ultimately took the new job.

Tip #2: Honor Yourself!

Butterfly daughters might be quick to judge themselves too harshly and question their own decisions. They wonder whether they've done everything they can to further their careers. They question whether they are staying in their chosen paths out of familiarity rather than a genuine sense of fulfillment. No one has the perfect career. I tell Butterfly daughters to stand by their values and trust their instincts because these judgments haven't let them down before. However, when women think they might have other interests that could lead to potentially greater career satisfaction, I encourage them to make time to explore these interests. It could be done through hobbies, classes, or a part-time job. Despite what many women may think, no one is trapped. We all have the ability to make the changes we want, small or substantial. If the choice is not to change at all, then that's okay too.

Tip #3: Honor Your Mothers!

Butterfly daughters, please express gratitude to your mothers. She gave you the gift and the ability to become yourself at an appropriate age. Other daughter types like the Ivy, Maverick, and Bootstrap daughters either had a slow process growing up or they grew up too fast. They were unable to move out of the shadows of the mother-daughter dynamic. Butterfly daughters, on the other hand, were able to mature at an appropriate pace because of their mothers' support.

Tip #4: Find Other Female Role Models

Butterfly daughters may not have been able to turn to their mothers to show them the way at work. That shouldn't limit an adult Butterfly daughter from seeking a female role model. Though we still live in a male-dominated world, there are more and more women who have successfully paved their own career paths. If there is a mentoring program at work, take part in it. Butterfly daughters can also turn to good friends and to other family members with similar experiences in their careers who can potentially guide them.

Tip #5: Challenge Pre-Conceived Notions

Not only are girls learning from mothers to understand their place in the professional world, they are also learning about the power dynamic between men and women. Butterfly daughters are at the forefront of challenging traditional notions, creating a dynamic that fits in with their professional and personal lifestyles. They can become leaders and mentors for future generations of women.

Tip #6: Find Your Voice -- and Be Heard

Butterfly daughters may not have acknowledged to themselves that they have doubts about their careers, career choices, or the level of leadership they wish to achieve. If this chapter provokes any new thoughts, a Butterfly daughter should listen to herself and find a way to express this. It is okay to be uncertain, and it is okay to say it out loud.

Chapter 5:

The Copycat Daughter

Tasha had the kind of career and lifestyle that many other women envied. At a young age, her mom, Kelly, would often take her to work. As she grew older, while her brother and sister went to the beach or hung out with their friends, Tasha chose to work at Kelly's office. She did any number of tasks, but mostly she filed, answered phones, and shadowed her mother at meetings. By the time she graduated high school, Tasha was certain that she wanted to work in the world of magazine publishing as well. Though her mother, Kelly, had many connections in that world, Tasha wanted to make it on her own. As the Editor-in-Chief of a high fashion magazine, Kelly was well-known for keeping celebrities, clients, and staff in line. Tasha had seen her mother in all of her "snake charming glory." Kelly could talk irate divas into letting the magazine publish articles or photographs that might be less flattering but more artistic. Kelly excelled at, and thrived on, the client interaction aspect of her job. Although she was a high achiever and competent in other areas, Tasha was tongue-tied and awkward around famous people; the thought of placating celebrities made her break out in a cold sweat. Although her mother offered her an internship opportunity at any fashion magazine of Tasha's choice, Tasha worked at a small independent literary magazine instead. The clientele there was low-key and more suitable for Tasha's temperament.

Tasha proved herself to be a capable, thoughtful and driven worker. She had good working relationships with managers, and coworkers also thought highly of her. People praised Tasha for her work ethic, her flexibility, and her willingness to chip in wherever needed. As a result, she quickly moved up the ranks of the literary magazine. After five years, Tasha was offered a Managing Editor opportunity at another literary magazine that was too good to refuse. By this time, her mother, Kelly, while continuing to be Editor-in-Chief of the fashion magazine, was featured on a local morning talk show as the "Beauty Guru." Because mother and daughter were very close, Tasha's name and face also became well known around town. Coupled with her excellent work performance and these connections, Tasha worked her way up to Editor-in-Chief at a prestigious and highly respected writers' journal. Several writers whose pieces she had handpicked for print received critical acclaim for their work. A few of them published books that made it onto *The New York Times* bestseller lists.

Tasha is a good example of a Copycat daughter, a woman with a successful career that closely resembles her mother's, although there are some subtle variations. What sets apart a Copycat daughter from the other daughter types in this book is that her mother was a role model for career success. She copies her mother's general career choices. That could mean getting involved in the family business or, like Tasha, specializing in a similar field. One of the reasons why Copycat daughters develop is because they share similar personalities, interests and skill sets with their mother. Copycat daughters are exposed to and immersed in their mothers' careers and interests during their entire lives. If the mother was involved in musical theater or the arts, she would likely take her children to performances or they'd often sing at home. Because a daughter's childhood was suffused with the creative arts, she has a predisposition to become a Copycat daughter. The likelihood of this happening increases when a daughter shares a talent with parents and sees how they enjoy their work.

Another common characteristic for Copycat daughters is that they are very close with their mothers and generally don't like to "badmouth" this relationship in front of others. Whenever I mention any of my mother's shortcomings, it doesn't sit well with me. I feel uncomfortable and awkward, as if I've somehow been caught doing something that is wrong. We all have a little Copycat daughter inside of us in that we inevitably emulate our mothers in some way. Copycat daughters can also understand the following situations: being seen as doing it all or having it all; trying to meet (real or imaginary) impossibly high standards; trying to equal their mother's accomplishments and feeling like they haven't or fearing that they've somehow disappointed her; feeling guilty if she has surpassed her mother; fearing her mother's real or imagined disapproval. Copycat daughters are generally fulfilled in their chosen line of work, despite a few inconveniences or discomforts. And so their career issues are not about starting over in a new field; in fact, the idea of starting over rarely crosses their minds.

To understand these women's career troubles, there must be a deep self-review of the past mother-daughter dynamic and, to a certain extent, of the present relationship. For example, "I can conquer the world" is a belief that a daughter may form from watching her mother break barriers at work. It's the same for negative beliefs like "I'll never measure up to her." Without self-review and without asking the tough questions, many women never realize why they hold their beliefs.

When things go wrong for a Copycat daughter, the problems are comparatively subtler than for other daughter types mentioned in this book. Going back to the psychological theory of development, we start our lives completely dependent upon our mothers (and fathers); as we grow older, we shift towards independence. Nobody is born a Copycat daughter. Just like height or shoe size, a woman's daughter type can change as she develops. A woman may be a Copycat daughter now, but she likely used to be an Ivy daughter (being very dependent) at some point in her past as well as a Maverick daughter (fighting that dependence). Instead of remaining in those stages, however, she naturally progressed beyond them. This is about consistent patterns of behavior, not the impetuous moment or two where an adult woman might have regressed to behave like a young child or a rebellious teenager. All women have these isolated moments. I also want to be clear that I'm not saying Copycat daughters don't feel dependent or rebellious. They do. But there is usually less visible drama. Copycat daughters might share interests or personality characteristics with their mothers, which may contribute to following in Mom's footsteps. These adult daughters had a road map for career and success. Superficially, they seem poised and in control of their careers, but underneath they may be holding in a reservoir of anxiety or uncertainty.

That was the case for Tasha. On the outside, life seemed as perfect as one's life can seem, but her close friends and family knew better. She was having trouble sleeping, was anxious all the time, and unable to fully relax. When people complimented her on how together her life appeared, Tasha felt like a fraud and that the cracks were beginning to form on the surface. At the end of one of my workshops at Tasha's company, Tasha took the initiative to follow up with me on some points I'd raised. She told me later that I had a very comforting presence which allowed her to make half-jokes about needing help managing her life. She was the quintessential "Super Mom," a successful senior magazine executive who managed a full-time job and a house with twin toddlers. We met and spoke several times more so that I could prepare a similar training for her department. During those times, Tasha mentioned that she had watched her mother, Kelly, run from her day job to her home job with a relentless amount of energy and grace. Tasha said her mother made balancing professional and personal obligations seem deceptively easy. It was only when she started her own family that she realized how difficult it really was. She wondered if times were different then. Tasha described her fear and insecurity about her career as a "heavy weight on her chest." Her mother was the epitome of self-assurance and competence. Tasha admitted, "I felt like I could never be like her."

Eventually, Tasha dropped the pretenses of speaking with me "for her employees' sake," and we began one-on-one counseling sessions in earnest. Early on, Tasha knew she wanted to pursue her mother's line of work, but she was also aware that she had no interest in pursuing her mother's exact line of work. That's why she chose not to work in the fashion world and instead spent the early stages of her career at literary magazines with small to medium circulations. There was a part of her that would have been perfectly content to continue working at small, independent companies. But Tasha also had a strong ambition to make a name for herself, just as her mother had done. Given her mother's success at work and our American work culture (that is, we emphasize individual achievements), it would have been strange for Tasha to turn down the opportunities offered to her. All of these factors compelled her to take on positions with increasing responsibilities at more prestigious companies. Though she was paid well and derived much satisfaction from her work, the increased work demands were taking a toll on her and on her time with her family. Even if she had her own huge workload, she was unable to say no when a colleague needed help finishing a project. She was overextending herself and didn't know how to stop. Also, Tasha was now forced to interact with the kind of high profile clients she had avoided in the past. On the nights before a meeting with a big client, worry prevented her from sleeping. She couldn't stop thinking about how much better her mother would have done it -- even if the meeting ended favorably for Tasha! She was beating herself up, believing that her mother was disappointed in her, because she could not accept the difference between herself and Kelly. Kelly was actually extremely proud of Tasha and saw great value in her daughter's different strengths. Tasha was a daughter who had built up her mom so much in her head that it was dragging her down.

Before adulthood, women go through three general stages of development: identifying with their mothers; realizing their individuality; and eventually disentangling their identities from their mothers to form one that is distinctly their own. This last stage is called separation, and, regardless of what kind of daughter you may be, it is usually the most difficult stage for both daughter and mother. I could write an entire book explaining why, but the essence of it is, while   young women must separate from their mothers to become their own selves, it's painful and difficult because we are born the same gender as our moms and are automatically regarded as extensions of them. In Yiddish, infant girls are sometimes called *mamela*, which means "little mothers." Not only does this suggest how she is "like mom" but can have the double meaning that when a mother calls her daughter *mamela*, she is somehow connecting her daughter to her own mother. This is just one of many subtle (and not-so-subtle) signs that direct women to remain close with Mom and learn her ways.

The degree to which we achieve separation from our moms (and how our moms achieve separation from us), reveals itself in how we deal with life, with love, and with work. My mother worked and raised children; that's how I knew I could manage a career and family too. When it is time for Copycat daughters to pursue a career, they tend to choose something similar to their role models because they assume that they too, have what it takes. While Tasha had separated from Kelly by choosing not to work in fashion, she was also still unconsciously identifying a little with her mom (by choosing to work as an editor in another industry). Just like Tasha, I too followed in my mother's footsteps in my own way. I didn't realize until much later how unusual it was to have started my own private practice so quickly after receiving my Master's degrees. While it typically takes years for other people to go out on their own, it had been a natural and intuitive next move for me. Many people asked how I had that kind of confidence at such a young age and with little experience. It was easy, I had seen my mother do it. Similarly, later on, when I asked my mother why she never talked to me about what it took to balance a family and a career, she said to me, "I didn't have to tell you. You saw me do it."

This sometimes contradictory combination of being one with and separate from Mom raises the odds that Copycat daughters will make satisfying and successful career choices. But it is a delicate balance. Overdependence and guilt can dominate when women are unable to separate from their mothers; rebellious actions and behaviors occur when they don't feel in control of their lives, decisions and paths. The balance is achieved when they begin to form their own, true career identities and understand the interests, skills, and values that might satisfy their desires. A mother's role in helping Copycat daughters become these (more or less) balanced career women is largely about showing them what's possible. As a working mom, her entire identity wasn't focused solely on the family unit. A mother of a young Copycat daughter who is growing up and moving beyond her mom's sphere of influence may experience less intense feelings of rejection. The mother had her own life, and thus she likely didn't feel the need to dictate how her daughter should lead hers. Having a professional life outside the home resulted in less compulsion to hold on too tight, which would have likely resulted in a Maverick daughter. At the same time, because the Copycat daughter was flexible and because a part of her was still closely connected to her mother's identity, it seemed a natural step for the adult daughter to choose a profession that was similar to her mother's. However, because of the very close relationship between Copycat daughters and their moms, when separation naturally occurs it can inflict a keen pain. A mother must deal with natural feelings of loss and grief when her daughter separates, and she will, because she knows it is best for her daughter. A few mothers of college-age daughters have vividly described the emptiness and loss when their daughters have gone off to college: "I truly knew what having a broken heart felt like. It feels like a death. I know that sounds morbid, but that was the worst thing, aside from someone dying. Then you just get used to living a different way. It's a big adjustment"; "I feel like my best friend left me and moved away"; and, "I literally feel like one of my body parts is missing when she's gone."

The Copycat daughter may want the world to see her as perfect and believe that anything less is a poor reflection not only on herself, but on her mother. It is another manifestation of the strong attachment she has with her mother's identity. In addition to being close with her mother, a Copycat daughter may place extra emphasis on her mother's approval or validation of her career choices. For instance, Tasha's mother, Kelly, took great care in being impeccably dressed. After all, she worked in the fashion world. Even though Tasha was not in the same industry as her mom, she still worked hard to maintain a perfect outward image. She didn't like leaving the house "underdressed," which meant no sweatpants or t-shirts, no clothing with holes or rips in it, and no unkempt hair. It meant spending significant time on her appearance before heading out the front door, even if it was a quick run to the supermarket for milk. Another example revealed that Tasha was still partially enmeshed with her mother's identify. During a 360-degree performance feedback (in which her employees evaluated Tasha's management skills), they rated her as a fair supervisor but also said she could be hard to approach and somewhat impersonal. Tasha was more than a little disappointed because her mom had maintained close friendships with many coworkers and subordinates. Tasha's anxiety around interacting with clients and troubled feelings from what her employees thought of her stem from her belief that not being exactly like Kelly was a letdown to her mother. Personally speaking, when my mom and I began leading mother-daughter workshops, I put pressure on myself because, between the two of us, I perceived Mom as the "uber-intellectual"! She spoke nine languages before learning English, and she was a psychoanalyst. I am sadly pathetic at languages and am a clinical career counselor. For the longest time, I perceived that my career was somehow less academic than my mom's. I had no reason to believe that; my mother and father had both been wonderfully supportive when I told them what I wanted to do. I was only able to let go of this nagging feeling after my mom complimented me on my hard work as a career counselor. She recognized that it might even be more difficult than being a therapist because my clients typically have concrete expectations, and they judge me by the yardstick of measurable outcomes.

This tendency for a Copycat daughter to compare herself to her mother becomes a push-and-pull: on the one hand, there is a competitive drive to achieve more than her mom; on the other hand, should that happen, feelings of triumph can give way quickly to regret and guilt -- as if she has somehow abandoned or betrayed her mother. In other chapters, I've talked about emotional landmines, automatic feelings or responses triggered by situations that seem similar to the ones we faced in the past. We tend to recreate the environment of our childhood, known as "repetition compulsion," by surrounding ourselves at work with familiar characters. For instance, there is someone who supports us, someone who annoys us, someone who seems hopelessly confused, and someone we consider a maternal figure. We do this, unconsciously, all the time. When Tasha first started working for Maureen, her current boss, she was terrified that she wasn't meeting Maureen's expectations. "When she would call me into her office, and we would disagree on how to approach a particularly complicated project, this tense knot would form in my stomach. I'd leave the office berating myself for not having seen it her way in the first place," she said. "There were so many times where I thought that Maureen must have regretted hiring me!" Poor Tasha was placing undue pressure on herself because in her mind, Maureen stood in as the maternal figure at work. It turned out there was a limit in how different Tasha wanted to be from her actual mom, Kelly, which transferred over to her work relationship with her boss, Maureen.

As a Copycat daughter, I've also transferred the maternal relationship onto my female boss. A few years ago, I

68

went on an interview for another job. Afterwards, I felt so guilty about it because I thought I was betraying my boss. She was a wonderful manager. She had been flexible by giving me the work-life balance that I needed; she had promoted me, and she had given me tons of support to get my work done. I thought, *how could I abandon her like this?* My husband, Jack, and others, reminded me that chasing after new opportunities was *normal*, and I would be unreasonable to confess that I'd had the interview to my boss, especially since I had already come to the conclusion that I had no interest in the job!

There is a dark side to being a Copycat daughter. A buildup of psychological havoc can accumulate from the self-imposed pressure of not being allowed to fail, of keeping up the appearance of a picture-perfect employee or boss, of the Copycat daughter's belief that she should be like her mother, and of her determination not to let anyone see any cracks on the surface. Without a healthy way of addressing impossible expectations, they can cause deep suffering and pain. Tasha's inability to leave the house perfectly groomed and dressed is an example. Another telltale sign for a Copycat daughter is if she has a hard time showing people her vulnerabilities because she believes it would somehow sully her reputation. Or perhaps she doesn't want to look at her dark side, and pretends it doesn't exist. What happens when a person refuses to accept the natural imperfections that we all have? She may find unhealthy ways to escape from them; at the extreme level, this could lead to abusing substances like alcohol or drugs. She may find herself feeling limited and overwhelmed, and, without intending to, may one day end up releasing a pent-up volcano of emotions.

We may consider a daughter who chooses to stay at home a Copycat daughter, if her mother also stayed home. Although this lifestyle is one that the Copycat daughter chooses, the pressure to live up to her mother's expectations remain. Those expectations may be about keeping up the home, raising the children, and any extra activities outside of the home. The stay-at-home Copycat daughter may not struggle with the decision to stay at home, she may struggle with self-confidence and finding purpose once her own children have grown.

Conclusion

As Charles Caleb Coulton said, "Imitation is the sincerest form of flattery." Copycat daughters grow up to follow in their mothers' footsteps. Their mothers were able to be role models for them both at work and at home. However, they may feel conflict in the instances when they are not *exactly* like their mothers and worry about not having their mothers' approval. Copycat daughters have big shoes to fill and footsteps to follow. The areas where they are not like their mothers can cause them to have self-doubt, especially if they revere, respect, or idealize their mothers' accomplishments. By reading this chapter, I hope Copycat daughters realize that they are not alone in feeling this way, and they don't have to keep holding onto their fears, anxieties, and concerns. If one were sitting before me right now, I would tell her the following: Don't be so hard on yourself. You don't always have to constantly strive to be good enough for Mom or any other person. You can learn to be kinder to yourself, to accept your flaws, to more fully appreciate the good in your life. To start, think about all the good things that make you uniquely you. Day by day, build on these things so that you can find your own way, approach, and strategy to realizing your career goals. In what ways can you create more fulfillment at work and better office dynamics? In what ways can you find the work/life balance that you crave? Whatever your solutions may be, also realize that this is not an overnight process. It will take time and patience. But knowing who you are and more fully appreciating your unique talents that are separate from your mother's are entirely worth the effort!

Tip #1: Pull Apart the Glue!

Because of the close connection between the two, sometimes it's difficult for a Copycat daughter to tell where she begins and her mother ends. Or why Mom's words and glances have such a strong hold. The good news is that this glue between a Copycat daughter and her mother and the resulting bond have given an adult daughter tremendous strength in her life. She can thank her mother for her self-confidence, knowing her place in the world, and her ability to take risks. The challenges come from the differences between mother and daughter, the areas where a daughter may experience self-doubt. If there is some emotional separation between these two women, the daughter may not not view those differences as some form of failure or shortcoming. When there is no emotional separation, the differences can cause the daughter so much pain that she may try to become more like her mother and move away from her own true interests. A healthy mother-daughter dynamic recognizes two distinct people, however tight the bond may be, as opposed to one being an extension of the other.

Tip #2: Own your career!
When Copycat daughters choose a slightly different path, this isn't a betrayal of their mothers. It may be scary, but, it's also natural. No two people can ever truly share all the same skills, interests, and desires. There is joy in diversity! It's a great goal for daughters to follow in their mothers' footsteps yet also maintain an identity of their own. Take the time to find those nuances and own them.

Tip #3: Show Your Vulnerability
Copycat daughters might have trouble showing vulnerability, especially to their mothers. Many of these women are conflicted when it comes to confiding in their mothers about the challenges in their lives. As much as they want their mothers to be aware and proud of their accomplishments, they also don't want their mothers to worry or be upset during tough times. What many daughters don't realize is that their mothers felt or feel the very same pressures about keeping up a strong front. Mothers don't want their daughters to worry, either. However, when

daughters take the initiative to open up to their mothers, they might find this out, and the relationship can grow even closer now that vulnerabilities are also being shared.

Tip #4: It's Okay to Think about Change
Our lives are constantly changing, and so are our priorities. If a Copycat daughter has a successful career that closely follows her mother's, she may hesitate when circumstances change and she can consider the option of staying home with children or switching careers. She wonders to herself: Am I throwing it all away? A Copycat daughter may feel more torn than others if she takes a different path than her mother, believing this somehow amounts to giving up on her mother. It is a double loss because the Copycat daughter realizes she is not a copycat any more, that she is moving in different directions from her mother. However, when an adult daughter makes the decision based on her own genuine interests, skills, values, and personality, she will feel relief, even if it is mixed in there with potential feelings of guilt and loss. My advice to Copycat daughters who are thinking about change is to embrace their new lives. We all have only one life to celebrate. In the long run, the relationships these women have with their mothers will remain intact even if their career choices are no longer the same. You don't have to be Mom's clone to remain close with her.

Tip #5: "Do Your Best" Is Good Enough!
Copycat daughters are hard on themselves. They have high standards to meet, having observed their mothers capably handle their careers and home lives. They believe they should also do as well. Despite how many daughters might feel, nobody is perfect. The biggest favor adult daughters might do for everyone around them (including their own mothers) is to acknowledge their own imperfections. As human beings, we all should strive to do better and to do the best we can. Sometimes we'll succeed,

and sometimes we won't. That's life and, more importantly, that's good enough!

Tip #6: Be Mindful of Mom's Inner Voice

Part of our early process with mother is incorporating her into ourselves. Sometimes, this can make it tough to differentiate the voices that pop into our heads. A Copycat daughter might think she holds an opinion, but upon deeper reflection realize that it's her mother's! This might be something as small as "don't take two weeks of vacation in a row, people need you at work", or something bigger like, "working in the hospitality industry is beneath you." When these strong opinions surface, take the time to wonder why, and from whom or where they come.

Tip #7: Wonder About the Work Dynamics

Many people unconsciously transfer their mothers' authority over to their women bosses. It can mirror the mother-daughter dynamic. Copycat daughters may feel great loyalty towards their bosses and are averse to disappointing them. The results can be women staying at a job longer than intended or being overly self-critical about their own limitations. If women have established such a dynamic with their women bosses, my advice is to separate Mom and boss from each other. Understand that your boss is not your mother, and pull off the emotional glue that might be holding you back.

Chapter 6:

The Bootstrap Daughter

Beth was affectionately referred to by her friends and family as "the one with a plan." They joked about how organized her life was and how she made a list for everything. At work, she could remember almost every scrap of paper that came across her desk. When she was on a project, she planned from a strategic viewpoint and was able to determine whether it could be effectively implemented on a local level. In fact, everything about her was efficient, from the way she prepared for meetings to the way she prepared for personal trips. Everything was always accounted for and had its place. It came as no surprise to people who knew Beth that she was valued at work and had a successful and stable career. Their response was, "That's so Beth."

Suffice to say, it came as a big shock when after seven years, Beth abruptly quit her job without a concrete reason. She told people that she wanted to explore her options. "People looked at me funny when I said that. They said it was so unlike me. But that's why I felt like I had to do it." What Beth did was extreme and against her nature; she needed to get away from the rigid constructs of her life. Although scary, it might have been a step in the right direction.

Beth was "the responsible one" in the family. When she was a child, her parents had very demanding jobs that kept them away from home most of the time. The responsibility fell on Beth, the middle daughter, to take care of the household and her brother and sister. From the time she was nine or ten years old, she made lunch for herself and her siblings to eat the next day at school. If there were any forms that needed to be filled out and handed in, she would look them over first. While her brother and sister did their homework, Beth cleaned the apartment and started dinner before her mother came home.

Beth and her family lived in a cramped one-bedroom apartment; she remembers there never being any space or privacy. It was also one of the reasons why her parents were often physically unavailable. When her mother, Maria, and father, Valencio, first immigrated to the United States, they lived in a neighborhood with a high crime rate. During their first three years in the country, their apartment had been burglarized twice. "When my parents moved to the States, it was like they were thrown into a pool of ice-cold water," Beth said. "They had a serious case of culture shock. My mom told me that they came from a small town in Ecuador, where community matters. You know, the kind of place where the neighbors watch each other's children and nobody's a stranger. Then they moved here, where everything has to be locked up and you need bars over your window."

Beth's parents decided that no matter what, they would live in a place where the young family would feel safe walking home at nights. To pay for housing in a safer neighborhood, Beth's parents took on multiple, low-paying jobs that kept them away from their children for long hours. As Beth grew older, she also became their de facto translator and go-between. She learned to translate legal and financial letters and helped her parents file their taxes each year. "It didn't occur to me," she said, "who did this work before me. I thought I was being a bad kid, if I said I'd rather hang out with my friends."

Beth and her mother, Maria, were close during her childhood and remain so today. Maria was always upfront with Beth about the household expenses and problems arising from them. "I don't know if other moms talked about money with their kids, but my mom did me a favor. Even though I now make a comfortable salary, I know how important it is to save and not to give in to outrageous impulse buys. I've got to live within my means." Maria encouraged Beth to find and take better opportunities available to her daughter that she never had. Beth did. She was the first in her family to graduate from college and remembers the big fuss Maria made over framing the degree certificate. Beth wasn't quite sure what to do once college was over. All she knew was that she had four years of student loans hanging over her head, and she wanted to start paying them off as soon as possible. She began temping as an office assistant at various companies. After a few months, she found a full-time, permanent position as an Administrative Assistant. Initially, Beth loved the job -- or, as she later recounts, the perks that came with it. "I was used to seeing my parents work long hours making half the amount I earned in a week. I had vacation and sick days! For the first time ever, I had health insurance."

Ironically, Beth couldn't bring herself to take advantage of the relatively shorter work hours and paid time off. "I am my mother's daughter," she said, ruefully. "Did I sometimes want to call in and take the day off? Use one of my sick days as a mental health day? Sure. But in the back of my mind, I would remember the times Mom had a 100-degree fever, and she still pushed that mop out the door to go clean someone's house." Beth subconsciously saw herself as an extension of her mother, to the degree that since her mother worked long hours, Beth expected to do the same as well. So she pushed herself relentlessly, staying late at the office to meet deadlines. She also resisted the urge to call in sick unless she couldn't get out of bed. Otherwise, she felt she'd be letting her mother down. "I know how much she and Dad sacrificed to provide for our family. I would never want them to think that I was ungrateful or unaware of what they had to do."

Due to her strict work ethic, supervisors were quick to assign her increasingly complicated tasks. She always made sure her assignments were turned in on time, regardless of her workload, and even asked if she could provide any additional assistance. She received promotions and offers to work elsewhere. Beth sometimes took those job offers if the work was interesting and the pay was higher. Despite this, she generally always left on good terms. By the time she was 32, Beth was an Executive Assistant for the CEO of an entertainment company. She put herself through college, paid off her student loans in five years, and used some of her vacation time to travel. What more could Beth possibly want?

It turns out, a lot more. For a while, being in a financially stable position seemed to be enough. Then, inexplicably, the work began to weigh her down. "I used to look forward to getting out of bed. I used to take pride in my work, but now I literally force myself to make the commute into the office. I think, 'If I get another email about this or that...' I hate it and I keep thinking maybe I just need... But then I don't know how to end that sentence. I don't know what I need and I don't know when these feelings of dread exactly began. It was little by little, until all of a sudden it was suffocating me." Beth's lack of enthusiasm began to seep through to her work. She forgot to block off time for a confirmed meeting, and mistakenly submitted a document full of spelling errors. Her supervisor didn't pay much heed to these mistakes because of her overall outstanding work record. Beth, however, berated herself over these mistakes enough for the both of them.

The term "bootstrap" comes from the lumberjack trade, where men hoisted themselves up trees using a strap wrapped around the trunk. They literally propelled themselves up. Today, it means being able to take care of yourself with little or no help from other people. Metaphorically speaking, Bootstrap daughters have hoisted themselves up into successful careers and lives. Unlike the Copycat or Butterfly daughters, their mothers usually were not role models for them in some way -- professionally, emotionally, or socially. There are many different reasons why a daughter is parentified at an early age. Perhaps her mother emigrated from another country; perhaps she was an alcoholic; perhaps her mother passed away. One daughter even described her mother as an emotional immigrant, due to her mental inability to navigate the world. Though their needs are not fulfilled, a Bootstrap daughter manages to thrive and become independent. But it's more than just self-sufficiency. Bootstrap daughters assume grown-up responsibilities at a young age. In Beth's case, she took care of her family when her mother and father were unavailable.

While Beth's mother could not give her any guidance in her chosen profession, Maria nonetheless provided her daughter with a foundation of emotional support, and, instilled in her a strong and unwavering work ethic. Not all Bootstrap daughters were exposed to this kind of maternal nourishment. Another client of mine, Jennifer, describes her mother in the following manner: "Gigi was the life of the party, but when the party was over, people went home and I got stuck with a hot mess." Because Gigi battled with alcohol and substance abuse dependencies all of her life, Jennifer assumed the caretaking role in the family between Gigi's numerous bouts of sobering up, falling off the wagon, and rehabilitating. For most of Jennifer's childhood, Gigi was unavailable for physical and emotional support. Since her mother was unable to hold onto a job for more than a few months, Jennifer worked 30 hours a week while managing an intense workload of advanced placement courses in high school. Jennifer was quick to sense when Gigi started using again -- she was used to catching the clues, habits and odd behavior that always followed. When that happened, Jennifer knew she had to lock away the valuables and cash, because Gigi would sell or spend whatever she could find in the apartment to satisfy her fix. With a mother who was unable to take care of herself much less others, and an absent father, Jennifer learned to look after herself, simply because she knew there was no one else on whom she could rely. This became evident to her, she told me, after she had been placed in the foster care system and was abused. While other children were worrying about homework or trying out for athletic teams or going to school dances, Jennifer worried about Gigi hiding bottles of liquor while simultaneously trying to keep Child Services at bay.

Though Beth's and Jennifer's stories are different, they have one thing in common -- they were both so busy taking care of their family needs that they missed a significant lesson during childhood, how to be children. It is during childhood that people have the chance to explore their interests in the most carefree manner possible. A child can fantasize about being a firefighter one day, a nurse the next, or a painter, musician, doctor, or lawyer. This exploration extends out of the play world and into the real one. Subconsciously, a child is making decisions and choices that will shape her personality, her behavior, and how she will move forward in life. People with a childhood that allowed them healthy amounts of exploration have a higher chance of growing into more mature, confident adults who are aware of their true self-interests. Beth and Jennifer were so preoccupied with grown-up issues, such as keeping the family intact, safe, sheltered, and nourished, that they probably missed opportunities to develop and explore during a critical time in adolescence. That's part of the reason why Beth may have felt so lost after college. She'd never thought about what she wanted to be when she grew up because she was too busy acting like a grownup while still a child. Like Beth, Jennifer's main concern after college was finding a job and building a life that was financially stable. It didn't even cross her mind to look for work that might be personally enriching or satisfying.

Many Bootstrap Daughters share some common strengths and characteristics. They tend to elicit the positive attention and support of teachers, mentors and other role models. They may be sensitive and in tune to unexpressed needs. Many may become caretakers and serve as emotional rocks for others. Some common places where they struggle include: being conflict-avoidant and lacking negotiation skills; pretending that everything is fine when it isn't; and, for daughters who grew up in a home with emotional instability, not knowing how to express anger or other negative feelings in a healthy manner.

The attributes that help a Bootstrap daughter succeed at work can also limit her. This harkens back to whether her needs were met or unmet by her mother. Jennifer's mom, Gigi, created a physical and psychic chaos around her, so Jennifer assumed the parent's role to clean up after that chaos, wherever and whenever possible. Today, Jennifer is a nurse at a hospice. While she's a favorite of patients, her colleagues feel differently. They consider her difficult. "People have described me as bossy and uptight," Jennifer said. "I will say it professionally, but I will say it. If someone is doing shoddy work to one of my patients, you're damn right I'm going to give you a piece of my mind. I don't care if you're the doctor or President!" Jennifer doesn't have many friends at work. The few people with whom she is friendly tell her that others describe her as snobby. "They say I turn my nose up at people, that I'm a bitch." Her reaction to this criticism is mixed. On the one hand, she is bothered by it more than she cares to admit. When she was telling me about what was being said behind her back, I noticed her mouth tightening and her body assuming defensive poses such as crossing her arms against her chest. Her irritation with criticism is further evident in how she responds verbally -- by becoming even *more* unfriendly. At the same time, she claims that she appreciates her own gruff manner: "I don't have to tell people twice to get something done."

Bootstrap daughters learned how to navigate people at a young age because they had to. Because of this, they can typically read a room and they make very effective leaders. They take charge and can navigate through work landmines. Although they're great at sensing tension in the air, Bootstrap daughters may have difficulty negotiating or expressing negative emotions that arise from these tensions. Many Bootstrap daughters want to shy away from conflict, which isn't surprising to me at all. As accomplished as these women are, many of them never fully developed the ability to talk things through, working out issues in an open and healthy way. Also, as exemplified in Jennifer's conflicted reaction to being called a snob, Bootstrap daughters tend to be sensitive to criticism. After all, they've been the "little grown up" for a long time, so they place a high value on being right all the time. This does not mean, however, that they are categorically inflexible. In fact, they often display high adaptability and flexibility in life situations, a trait they needed and used to deal with the uncertainties they faced in their childhoods. While this usually works to their advantage in the workplace, it can be extremely detrimental and emotionally trying when they don't have an answer or when, heaven help them, they make a mistake. In personal relationships, this may also come across as being overly judgmental or stubborn.

The coping strategies of an adult Bootstrap daughter developed when she was a small child. They served their purpose by meeting otherwise unfulfilled needs, but she is not aware that these coping strategies are no longer necessary in her adult life. For example, Jennifer never told Gigi how much suffering she endured whenever Gigi relapsed. "It wasn't a picnic for her either," Jennifer said. "I could see how much she struggled with not using. I always wanted to be strong for her." Instead, Jennifer held onto her rage because she knew that expressing it would not be welcomed or acknowledged. Whether she was conscious of it or not, Jennifer learned that her feelings didn't matter, and she also learned that she was to blame when things went wrong. Now that she's an adult, Jennifer has a learned, automatic response to hold back during tense or uncertain situations. Sometimes this builds to an uncontrollable rage or guilt, and she feels like she wants to explode.

Again and again, the biggest stumbling block for adult daughters is the concept of being separate from their mothers. Separation differs by varying degrees between each daughter (and between each category of daughter). For most Bootstrap daughters, the anxiety over separation stems from their over-parentification as children. Their mothers simply weren't able to take care of themselves, much less their children. For Beth, this surfaces in the guilt she feels when she wants to call in sick. For Jennifer, her decision to choose a stable job was a direct reaction to Gigi's inability to remain gainfully employed. Though their childhood experiences were different from one another's, the underlying questions for both Jennifer and Beth are: "Do I really like what I do? Am I paying for my mother's past regrets, her disappointments or letdowns? Do I have a choice in what might make me professionally fulfilled?"

Conclusion

Bootstrap daughters may believe that their childhood experiences fostered more independence, and that is true. However, their childhoods also reflect an unnecessary burden on the children that they were, and places an undue burden on the women they are now. Growing up, they may have held greater authority in some respects (doing the taxes), but they were also powerless (feeling or being blamed, if their brothers and sisters didn't pass their math tests). Sometimes this discomfort is tolerable and therefore they don't challenge their unnecessary burdens for many years, if ever. Women who are Bootstrap daughters may not even be conscious that this is a source of pain. A vital first step a Bootstrap daughter must take in order to understand her triggers and realize her potential is to recognize that she is no longer the over-parentified child she once was. Despite what she's come to believe, the world does not weigh upon her shoulders. She can let go of some of the responsibilities and confront the unconscious, irrational, early childhood experiences linked to change. She should remind herself that she does possess the requisite strengths and abilities to deal with her adult reality. Perhaps her journey in adulthood is to capture elements that were minimized in her childhood.

To help Bootstrap daughters achieve the change they seek, one of the most important steps is the acknowledgment that they have room to grow. Having played the adult since childhood, they perceive certain behaviors and circumstances as being etched in stone. For a long time, Beth was unable to justify switching to a new career because, while she was dissatisfied, she was not unhappy. She learned at an early age to sacrifice her own needs and desires. To break this habit, Beth had to acknowledge the discomfort of not being in sync with herself. She -- and all Bootstrap daughters -- can't make excuses just because the pain is minimal. She must look for the subtler cues that suggest her career could be more satisfying.

Now that you have read descriptions of all five daughter types, you will see that you may identify with one or more simultaneously. Though Beth is primarily defined as a Bootstrap daughter, she could also identify with a Butterfly daughter. Bootstrap Jennifer could simultaneously be an Ivy daughter depending on how her needs and pain manifest themselves. Consider the main gist of these daughters, and realize that you may not identify with every facet of a particular type. That's okay. We are complicated beings and the categories are designed and defined to help you think more deeply about your personal situation, rather than putting you in a box. Likewise, pick and choose the tips and solutions throughout the book which you think might work best for you instead of sticking only with those suggested for a particular daughter type.

Tip #1: All in Good Time

Bootstrap daughters don't typically make rash decisions but rather take their time to transition professionally. They appreciate their security, weigh risks carefully, and will move to a new job or career, if it makes sense. They should be careful not to compare themselves to others who have an easier or faster time moving out or moving on. Their thoughtfulness with transitions will pay off.

Tip #2: Manage Maternal Expectations

Bootstrap daughters had to "parent" their mothers to some extent, and now Mom may not understand why her daughter is experiencing career woes. Mothers may also not be able to give their daughters the feedback, recognition, or praise they seek when taking on a risk such as making a career move or succeeding at work. I tell Bootstrap daughters that their mothers might not understand right away or ever. Instead, I encourage these daughters to look to others to celebrate them and provide needed feedback.

Tip #3: Relax! You are not responsible for everyone!
Bootstrap daughters who are still taking care of their mothers (and maybe fathers) may feel resentment over time about this care. In order to release this resentment, Bootstrap daughters must release themselves of the responsibility they feel for others. They must learn how to live their lives. Otherwise, Bootstrap daughters are at risk not only for resenting family members, but also for giving up their dreams.

Tip #4: Use Your Special Powers!
A Bootstrap daughter who has, or had, an alcoholic mother (an adult child of an alcoholic or ACOA) may think the only influence this has on her work is a negative one. But these Bootstrap daughters probably spent a great deal of time learning how to be sensitive to moods. They develop a keen sensitivity to social cues when entering a room and assessing the moods and tensions of those around her. Although these women may no longer be taking care of an alcoholic mother, the skills they developed can work favorably in positions of management and leadership. Use them! This subtle information can help Bootstrap daughters make decisions and understand team dynamics.

Tip #5: Model Mentors
Bootstrap daughters excel at seeking out, finding, and developing great relationships with other women who give excellent advice, mentor and serve as role models. They should not be shy about recognizing this as a strength, and should continue to use this resource in furthering their careers. In turn, they can serve as great mentors, facilitators, and advocates themselves.

Chapter 7:

A Family Affair

"We all grow up with the weight of history on us. Our ancestors dwell in the attics of our brains as they do in the spiraling chains of knowledge hidden in every cell of our bodies."

-Shirley Abbott

"The family. We were a strange little band of characters trudging through life sharing diseases and toothpaste, coveting one another's desserts, hiding shampoo, borrowing money, locking each other out of our rooms, inflicting pain and kissing to heal it in the same instant, loving, laughing, defending, and trying to figure out the common thread that bound us all together."

-Erma Bombeck

Fathers. Siblings. Grandparents. Uncles. Aunts. Cousins. Most of this book has focused on trying to answer the question, "What's Mom still got to do with it?" This chapter explores the other family relationships in the adult daughter's life. We can't discount how their roles may have influenced women's personalities and career choices. There can be hundreds, if not thousands, of decisions and choices that a woman makes along the way which shapes her career. Her decisions can be influenced by so many people from her family and life.

These days, families come in different shapes and sizes. Many daughters grow up in a single-parent household; they may have two dads or two moms; they may have stepparents or perhaps were raised by family members other than their mothers or fathers. There are all kinds of nontraditional families. In the next section, I review basic ideas about some of these dynamics and how they relate to Ivy, Maverick, Butterfly, Copycat, and Bootstrap daughters.

Fathers and Daughters

Traditionally and historically, fathers have been perceived as the less involved caregiver since they were usually out in the workforce while women stayed home. This stereotype is rapidly changing, as evidenced in the rise of household products advertisements aimed at fathers. For example, a recent television commercial showed a young father in a minivan picking up his son and friends from baseball practice. The ad then switched over to a scene at home where the father was cleaning dirty uniforms at the washing machine and later feeding the rowdy group of boys at the kitchen table. This changed perspective could be due to several factors. First and foremost, there's been unprecedented growth in opportunities for women -- educationally, professionally, and socially -- in the past 50 to 75 years. Also, with the necessity for two-income households, society has had to rethink what's traditionally considered "women's work." It's important to acknowledge that despite the change with many more women in the workforce, and an increased expectation that men help within the household, there is research that supports that women continue to have the lion's share of the housework and family management responsibilities.

My focus on the role of fathers is to explore how they influence their daughters' career choices. The stronger her bond is to her father, the more a woman may identify with his career path. This is a bit of a generalization, as the bond between father and daughter can also be complex. His influence is more apparent when the mother-daughter

86

dynamic is off-balance. If she is a Maverick daughter and has a volatile relationship with her mother, she may regard her relationship with her father as the stable one. He may be the peacemaker, and she may confide in him more; in turn, she may see him as more of a role model and be more open to his career choices than she would be to her mother's. (Remember, Maverick daughters are likely to rebel and do the opposite of their moms, even if it's to their own detriment.) Ivy daughters, whose needs were greater than their moms could meet, may have had fathers who provided the additional support, attention, or other resources. As for Bootstrap Daughters, it is likely that she had to parent not only her mother but also fulfill a parenting role for her father, too. Bootstrap daughters who grew up with a disabled or alcoholic mother may resent their fathers for not doing more to protect them.

All families have dynamics - some healthy, some not. Whatever the family dynamic may be, a daughter is carefully watching both of her parents' behaviors and choices. She is picking up the subtle and obvious clues about a woman's role in the home, in the workplace, and in particular her power (or lack thereof) in the home. If the male has more power in the parental partner relationship, the daughter may reject that aspect of her mother for fear of becoming powerless or subordinate to men. She may be angry at her mother for not standing up to her father, and she may want to identify with her father as the "strong" one in the family. Daughters can reject some aspects of their mothers and accept others. However, because daughters are trying to figure out from a very young age how they will be "just like mom" (or not at all), and because they are the same gender, daughters may be particularly sensitive to their moms' limitations, especially their weaknesses.

Looks and genetics can also be interesting elements to explore in the father-daughter dynamic. If a daughter "looks just like her father" or "acts just like her father," she is likely to adopt more of her father's legacy. There is great power in the words we say and hear. When a daughter hears throughout the years, "Oh, you'll grow up and be just like your dad, you're a carbon copy of him," it can turn into a self-fulfilling prophecy.

It is important to realize that the mother-daughter relationship does not exist in a vacuum. The father plays an important role in the dynamic, and subsequently in the daughter's decisions. His absence also impacts a daughter's career. It is not uncommon for a mother to raise her daughter alone, whether it is due to the death of a spouse, divorce, or the mother's decision to remain single by choice. In these instances, the mother-daughter relationship is more intense because they really only have each other. The dynamic is magnified, and the daughter has fewer role models.

When the mother-daughter relationship is healthy and functionally supportive, and when the family unit is a cohesive one as a whole, the father's role may serve to underscore and supplement the examples that a mother sets. He may be the guiding hand, if a mother does not have the requisite career experiences to serve as a career role model. Whatever the case may be, a father should not be viewed as irrelevant to his daughter's career development, regardless of the relationship between her parents or the parental living arrangements.

Siblings

Some social psychologists believe that birth order is an important factor in shaping personalities. One of the leading voices in this theory is Alfred Adler, a contemporary of Sigmund Freud. Adler believed that families are constellations: each member is a star with its own gravitational pull, exerting force and being exerted upon. With the addition of new and successive stars, the dynamic of the constellation inevitably changes. That is, each child in a family is likely to be raised differently by the same parents (due to their gained experience in child-rearing, as well as the additional knowledge and resources parents pick up as the family grows). With firstborn children, parents may be more fastidious: they read about what to expect during their firstborn's childhood and development, and follow current trends of childrearing accordingly. With subsequent children, parents may be more relaxed and may make different decisions than those made while raising their first one. Often, two sisters will not identify as the same daughter type. Each daughter's relationship with her mother is unique to that duo. A mother parents each child differently because of where she is in her own life when her children are born. In addition, each child comes with his or her own temperament, personality, and dynamic with mother and father. So the women in a family with multiple daughters will likely identify with different daughter types.

Losing a Family Member and Its Effect on Adult Daughters
When there is a loss of a family member, not only is there grief and mourning on a personal level, but it can have an effect on an adult daughter's career choices too. My experience with clients who have lost a sibling suggests that they feel a significant pressure to fulfill the unrealized dreams that the deceased brother or sister had. In terms of career, the unfulfilled dreams and aspirations of the deceased become legacies for the surviving daughter. This is an important dynamic worth mentioning and part of the career puzzle for women who have lost a sibling. The adult daughter feels three key expectations when she has lost a sibling: meeting her parents' expectations; meeting her own expectations; and, meeting expectations she attributes to the lost sibling. All of these expectations tend to be unspoken and are probably unconscious.

Other Family Members
It's also important to acknowledge the presence of other caregivers, influencers, and role models in non-traditional families, such as same-sex couples/marriages, multi-generational families being raised together, and other types of family/community units. The mother-daughter relationship also has to be considered in the context of other members of the family. There may be less pressure or focus

on this relationship, if a girl has two lesbian mothers, or in the case of three generations of women living together. For example, the grandmother-mother link can have a profound impact on the mother-daughter relationship. The daughter might develop empathy for her mother after watching how her mother is treated by her grandmother. Alternatively, several daughters may claim that they are just like their grandmothers.

If a daughter has lost her birth mother, or if her parents have divorced, a stepmother may also provide, at least in terms of the daughter's career, the mothering and role modeling a daughter needs. If a woman did not receive sufficient mothering at a young age, she is likely to develop into an Ivy or Bootstrap daughter.

Whatever the arrangement is in the family unit -- a daughter's mother and father lived together or separated, or other unique family circumstances tempered her past -- it is important to consider the full picture and all the relevant influences in her life. Each person, to a certain degree, imparts on a daughter his or her critical legacies -- implicit and explicit messages about career and life choices, role modeling, and the values that lie deep within all of us. These factors can be a guiding light or a force with which to be reckoned. My experience indicates that an adult daughter will carry these messages and factors with her throughout her life.

Chapter 8:

Okay, So Now What?

After hearing stories like Veronica's, Gillian's, Sofia's, Tasha's, and Beth's, it is, hopefully, apparent that mothers have an indelible impact on how we women think, look, and act in our professional lives. Our mothers' influence on us is powerful and long lasting. For those who may feel overshadowed by their mother's influence, the challenge is to take the best from what their mothers had to offer while no longer allowing what doesn't work to get in the way. Some of the work will require a deep exploration of one's relationship with Mom; some of it will require an adult daughter to have a potentially uncomfortable and unflinchingly honest review of her job, career, or the challenges that she faces. It may take some women a long time to act on the recommendations for moving forward, but others might be able to start right away. It is a time for critical and deep self-reflection. Women must try to be honest about their relationships with their mothers. It's not uncommon for us to place our moms on impossible pedestals: she is either the saintly, do-no-wrong superwoman or, as I've overheard other women say, "evil incarnate." When we think in black-or-white terms in describing any person or situation, we should take the time to wonder why. This might be a sign that there is a lack of separation in a mother-daughter relationship.

The truth is, mothers are all complicated human beings, just like everyone else. A mother might have been and probably was very good with her daughter in some ways and lacking in other ways, both supportive and critical. Just like her daughter, she struggled with life choices in balancing her needs and inner desires for a fulfilling career with the demands of raising a family. At whatever age or whichever stage in her life, she is a vulnerable daughter with her own unfinished business and her own needs. She is also playing out the dynamics from her own childhood/daughtering.

I'm reminded of Amy Tan's book, *The Joy Luck Club*, and the description of the dynamics between generations of women in a family: "I was taught to desire nothing, to swallow other people's misery, to eat my own bitterness. And even though I taught my daughter the opposite, still she came out the same way! Maybe it is because she was born to me and she was born a girl. And I was born to my mother and I was born a girl. All of us are like stairs, one step after another, going up and going down, but all going the same way." This passage, spoken from a mother who deliberately tried to raise her daughter with different expectations only to see her turn out the same way, reveals the odd paradigm women face: our personalities, behaviors and reactions can be complicated reflections of our relationships with our mothers that extend into past and future generations. Our threads with our mothers, grandmothers, and daughters are woven together in a tapestry - distinct from one another but at the same time inseparable. Threads can cross and touch threads that have come before or after. The task is to try to find ways for a woman to recognize her own thread and the value and unique contribution she brings to the tapestry.

As mothers and daughters, we women can spend a lifetime working out our unfinished business and unmet needs. Becoming a mother does not resolve the issues. Instead, those issues can end up unconsciously imbued into other people -- probably those who are closest to a mother, including her daughters, friends, and even coworkers. Think about how much time is spent at work. The people at work become extended members of each other's families. The mother-daughter dynamic that a woman grew up with not only affects her career choices and development, but her interpersonal work life as well. There is a general belief that adults have their acts together, as opposed to children who are less able to hide their needs. But that's exactly what hinders adults today: we stow away our perceived deficiencies with far more skill than children. We may even consciously forget about them, but the issues themselves do not fade away. What might have been small wounds back then have now become much more problematic for our adult selves. Our lack of awareness means that these issues can come out in how we perceive the work that we do, our relationships, our self-esteem, how we interact with other women, and in many other ways.

Sometimes, it's not about unmet needs. Sometimes, even when a mother tried to meet all of her daughter's needs, her daughter's needs were met too much. The Maverick daughter, whose mother tried to "over"-meet her daughter's needs, ends up rebelling for the sake of rebellion while forsaking sources of satisfaction that linked back to her mother. Nobody likes to be controlled, and over-mothering is controlling. All daughters have an inherent need for space and autonomy. And even when mothers seem to provide well-balanced mothering, there is still the chance that it isn't enough or it's too much. There's no perfect mothering formula because a daughter, her mother, and the generations of women preceding and following them are all different, even given their similarities. This variance in temperament, genetic makeup, personalities, skills, interests, and a woman's role in the family dynamic is what makes her unique.

In fact, it's very likely that mothers don't identify with the same daughter type as their children do. Many women are surprised at this, which underscores my point throughout the book about the lack of separation between many daughters and their mothers. This close connection can continue to influence women by prompting opposite behaviors. For example, a Maverick daughter who still might struggle with having a controlling mother will be inclined to do the opposite with her own daughter.

So let's get started – there's much that we can accomplish together!

People want to have a memorable life that has meaning, which includes feeling connected to others and not being isolated. When you consider how much of our lives are spent in pursuit of work, finding a job that is enriching and satisfying is of paramount importance. People who are happy at work tend to be connected to their jobs and careers. Not only do they take ownership of it, they are fully engaged and energized by it. To reach this level of career satisfaction takes an honest self-inventory of your interests, skills, values and personality. This self-assessment works when you're able to filter out most of the extraneous noise of the complicated past, your present situation, or your future fantasies. Once we become in tune with our true selves, we begin to attain a better understanding of what motivates and invigorates us. It will astonish you how clear things can become and where your true talent lies. Finding a career that matches your talents and interests, versus one that doesn't, is the difference between trying to write with your right hand when you are left-handed, or wearing shoes that fit rather than pinch your toes.

People may believe they don't have the time or resources to make key changes in their lives, but this view prevents them from pursuing what could make them very happy. Although there is compromise involved, when you know what you want to do and you know how to get there, the pros far outweigh the cons. People who find their true calling enjoy going to work every day. In fact, if they couldn't earn a living doing what they love, they would still continue doing it for free. When we understand who we are, what makes us tick, the things we enjoy and excel in, and the things that truly matter to us, we can begin to make decisions based on who we are and what we want.

My Counseling Philosophy and Approach

Many people ask how understanding their past can help them create their best professional future. When clients come to me for career counseling, they are unhappy with and having repetitive problems in their careers. They may be experiencing anxiety, depression, or some other mental health issue interfering with their careers. They may have difficulty finding meaningful work. Often they are bored, frustrated, or feel like they never answered the question: "What do I want to be when I grow up?" Clients come to me because they have career dissatisfaction. Before meeting with me, many people have made a number of common but unsuccessful attempts at resolving issues at work. They may look online to see the types of jobs that are available for them. Internet searches don't fix the problem. Instead, people feel overwhelmed, under-qualified, and, invisible as well as discouraged. That's because online job searches are often not successful due to the low rate of employer response. While it is a wonderful resource, other work needs to be done before people start looking online.

Another unsuccessful attempt frequently made by people before they come to me is rushing from career dissatisfaction straight to a resolution. It is much easier to rush a decision and go on the path of least resistance than to take the time needed for fully exploring and identifying the blockages to satisfying work. Examples include: taking the first job they are offered; choosing a major without much thought; or doing anything that's different in an effort to relieve their career pains. But, as with any major decision in a person's life, it is much better to move to something wonderful than it is to merely move away from something painful. The third mistake that people make is getting stuck and not making any changes for a very, very long time because they don't know what else to do. This approach is aptly described by the saying: "Better the devil you know than the devil you don't know."

The career approach that I advocate, and which I have seen yields the best results in my twenty-five years as a practicing career counselor, is when people refrain from making impulsive decisions and instead spend the time to fully explore their selves as well as their world of work.

People need to truly understand their internal career profile, which includes taking a look at their interests, skills, values, and personality. After a person has completed this internal search, she'll have an easier time exploring career options in the external world. She will be more adept at identifying what is a good fit for her.

In addition, we all have unique internal barriers that can hold us back from reaching resolution or career satisfaction. Examples of internal barriers include: our fears; issues; anxieties; and, depression. Counseling can help people become more aware of how internal barriers are contributing to unsuccessful career transitions. Unresolved issues in the mother-daughter dynamic left over from childhood may be one source of these barriers. When these internal barriers manifest themselves, particularly due to the dynamic a daughter had or has with her mother, women may get stuck. This could involve an inability to make decisions or find true self-interests or a role model. When adult daughters are unable to propel themselves forward, counseling can help. Even when women know what they want, they must work hard to stand out in competitive job searches. A person can review all the essential skills, interests, and personality factors that she wants, but if she is stuck, she should consider how her dynamic with Mom might be holding her back.

In the following section we're looking at four aspects of self-assessment. We'll take a look at the main factors that help people identify potentially satisfying careers. Take the time to carefully consider the information presented and start to think how you can apply it towards your own career. There may be other factors not on the list but, in my experience, the ones below have the greatest impact on our career paths.

Interests Are the Things People Enjoy Doing

I describe interests as the things that we all like to do and make time to do during our spare time. Out of all the building blocks of career satisfaction, this is one where, as children, we exerted the most amount of control and independent decision-making. We may not have had any say in the matter of pursuing an education as children, but many of us were encouraged to develop interests outside of school. These interests are wide and diverse -- you may have developed a fondness for reading comic books, growing cacti, or playing the cello. Many children are given the opportunity to play sports. I ask my clients to think about what their interests were back then and what they are now. Sometimes they are stumped for an answer so I try these other questions as well: Are there any hobbies that have followed you from childhood into adulthood? Are there any hobbies that you wished you had pursued and are not quite sure why you didn't? Do you find yourself gravitating towards one subject over another? More specifically, when you're reading a magazine or surfing the web, what articles or topics always grab your attention? If you visit a bookstore without a specific agenda, which sections are you most interested in? Look at your circle of close friends and family. Do you talk about or share similar interests with any of them? The important thing about interests is that people voluntarily choose to do these things in their free time. People may even be spending their hard-earned dollars to fuel these hobbies. Therefore, it may be worthwhile to consider the possibility of turning the things people love to do into some type of professional practice that pays. For those who think it is unrealistic or impractical to align their careers with a hobby or interest, I encourage them to consider better alignment with the industry in which they work or the people with whom they work. Though I have spent years working with artists and designers, I know that I will never become one. I also know that I love being surrounded by creative people who think out of the box. I encourage all of my clients to find and be around their type of people.

Skills Are What People Are Good At

There are three types of skills that I talk about with my clients. The first type is content specific skills, or things that people learned in school or on the job. This could be a particular software program, the technical expertise needed to become an engineer or doctor, or speaking another language. The second type is self-adaptive skills, which is how we carry ourselves through life. Some examples of self-adaptive skills include how we present ourselves in front of others, whether we are punctual for meetings, or the way we respond in difficult situations. The last type is transferrable skills, which are important to identify during a person's career transition period. These are skills easily transferred from one industry or job to the next. Whether a person works on the trading floor of the New York Stock Exchange, as a retail sales clerk, or teaching in a classroom, these skills will rise to the top no matter where she works. Transferrable skills are not limited to one area of work. To name a few, they can include communication, leadership, analytical or physical skills, data organization, research, advising, and teaching. It's crucial for everyone to tap into their most natural skills at work so that they are energized rather than drained by it.

Nature has endowed us with the potential for certain skills that fit our unique personalities. It's so important for people to tap into their "motivated" skills and natural capabilities. These skills can be both innate and learned as we mature. Our mothers also served as role models for learned skills. They might have passed down skills to us such as bookkeeping, playing an instrument, cooking or talents in many other areas. If a mother had strong ideas about living and working spaces not being too cluttered, then her daughter probably is acutely aware of that too. Whether or not an adult daughter chooses to act on this preference is a different matter. Take Tasha from the Copycat daughter chapter. Her mother had the self-adaptive skill of being presentably dressed when leaving the house. In turn, Tasha did the same too, to the point where she thought wearing jeans was too casual for a quick run to the supermarket. Like Tasha's mother, all our mothers knowingly or unknowingly might have pushed us towards certain skill sets and preferences.

While the daughter types in this book do not limit women to certain skill sets, they may increase awareness of particular capabilities and help determine what women choose to do with these capabilities. A Copycat daughter may expect to have similar skills as her mother's if she follows the same or similar career path. Tasha and her mother Kelly worked in publishing, but while Kelly was great interacting with clients, Tasha was not. Tasha's anxieties at work involved Tasha thinking that she was not meeting her mother's expectations. For a long time, she wasn't able to recognize that she had a different personality from her mother and didn't know how to accept that.

Bootstrap and Butterfly daughters like Beth and Sofia may feel guilty about exceeding their mothers' skills. They had to learn to accept that guilt, even when they may have been expected to excel. For Butterfly daughters, their mothers may have instilled the belief that their daughters are capable of doing anything. Ivy and Maverick daughters like Veronica and Gillian may be unaware of their skills and will need help in identifying them. At every first session I have with a client, I ask her to name her strengths. It never ceases to surprise me how often women clients can't tell me or have difficulty articulating their specific skills. They are literally at a loss for words. For these women, part of the work is naming all of these strengths, which help to build their self-confidence. It is not enough for a woman to say, "I know I have good people skills." She should be able to say that she is a good listener, that she can develop trust and rapport, along with other specific descriptors.

A client of mine, whom I'll call Shirley, wanted to transfer from her client-centric sales position at the company where she had worked over five years into a back office position that focused more on data generation and analysis. When Shirley finally transferred to the position she desired, however, she was overwhelmed by the high quota of data entry that the position demanded. Suddenly, she had no time to do anything else but process forms. Shirley was a friendly woman who had formed congenial relationships with her clients. They tended to call her for assistance even if the help they needed could come from another person or department. Shirley thought she wanted a change, but she didn't do well focusing on one type of task and one alone. She liked variety in her day, and she missed talking to and seeing her clients. She was never so grateful as the she was the day that her supervisor transferred her back to her sales position, where she happily remains today. Shirley did not think through the significance of this move; she had no basis to judge the outcome and did not even know how to ask the questions. Shirley's story is an example of how important it is to understand one's strengths and work in a job or role that taps into one's best skills. Shirley's motivation was a promotion, but then she was unhappy when her skill set didn't match the new job.

If, however, a woman had a mother who was a role model, she has a higher chance of understanding her own skills and where they can be developed. At any age, we have the wonderful ability to learn how to view our skills or strengths differently - and to apply them towards different careers. It's never too late to reinvent yourself. J.K. Rowling, the author of the wildly popular Harry Potter series of books and movies, didn't become a published writer until after she had been a researcher, a bilingual secretary, an employee in the Chamber of Commerce, and a teacher of English. Although a person may not change her analytical, technical, and other inherent strengths, her capacities stretch wider than she believes. The nuances are many, and women are encouraged to focus on different aspects for different careers. The goal for women is to own what they have, articulate it, and put it out in the world.

Evie was told her whole life that she was terrible with details. She couldn't balance her checkbook and was notoriously late for meetings because she could never remember the locations. But that was only true about certain aspects of Evie's life. When it came to things she cared about, she was incredibly precise. Evie's interests lay in biological sciences and chemistry. She wanted to pursue a career in pharmaceutics, but a nagging voice inside her head told her that she might kill someone, if she filled a prescription incorrectly. Compound that nagging voice with the pain Evie felt watching her mother go through a medical malpractice suit. If you were Evie, how much of these fears would factor into the decision to go to pharmacy school? In witnessing a mother's difficulties, most daughters may be strongly affected because of the mother-daughter dynamic, and they'll find it hard to get over their mothers' ordeals. Such scenarios affect how daughters see themselves, as they invariably feel like an extension of their mothers, and Moms' issues could potentially shape many decisions of their daughters. Many women, like Evie, don't trust their own skill sets.

When women are aware of their skills, they can open up their potential for themselves and for their employers. Identifying those skills may take some time, though, and for women who don't know where to start, I pose these questions: Besides the areas you excelled at in school, what did you enjoy doing outside of class? What did you need to know, and how did you learn to do these things? Can any of the skills that you developed carry over into your work life? Consider signing your name with your non-dominant hand and then with your dominant hand. Although you can learn to write with the non-dominant hand, you will always need to think harder, expend more energy, and it will cause you more strain. It's the perfect analogy in identifying skills that come most naturally to us.

For women who are thinking about, or who have started to change their jobs or careers, it can be a scary and overwhelming time. It's normal for people to think the following: *What if I can't hack it? What if I don't have the experience? What if I fail spectacularly?* To help keep fears at bay, I encourage them to take an inventory of their skills and apply those skills toward their new profession. I also help women learn to communicate this value to themselves and to potential employers. A person might find out that she is better equipped to handle the new challenges than she initially believed.

Values Are What's Important in Life.

Our values are shaped by our parents, the society in which we live, and the decisions we made or were made for us as children. We make decisions based on the values that are important to us in life. Money, independence, personal achievement, and recognition are examples of values that we absorbed from the people around us. Unlike interests and the things we enjoy, we had minimal control over what values were imparted to us. When our values and interests don't align or directly conflict with each other, it causes many of us to stumble in our careers. If a woman's interests involve helping the impoverished but her values place heavy emphasis on financial success, she faces a tough choice. It's a complicated push-and-pull.

The value that many of us place on money is a critical component in the shape of our career paths. At one point or another, we have probably heard the following ideological beliefs: "Never be dependent on a man"; "Money doesn't grow on trees"; "You should marry someone who can support you financially"; "Money makes the world go round"; "You have to spend money to get money"; "Save a penny to earn a penny"; "What are you saving your money for? You should enjoy your life right now"; and "Why are you throwing your money away? You have to save for your retirement." Children hear these conflicting messages, often from the same people, so it's confusing. They usually grow up with some garbled interpretation incorporating some or all of these beliefs, which influences their career choices. Some may choose a stable if mentally unstimulating job for financial security, while others pursue hard work for little or no financial reward.

Other values are so deeply ingrained that we may not even be aware of how they could differ from our parents' values and from society in general. These values stem from cultural, religious and socioeconomic backgrounds. Should mothers stay home to take care of their children? If they work, should they choose less demanding jobs that won't distract them from focusing on their families? Many people wind up in careers that they believe they want or that their parents want for them. Daughters may fulfill their mothers' unfulfilled dreams. Some cultures or societies expect daughters to not only surpass their moms but to support them when they retire; other daughters are dependent on their moms or parents many years after becoming legal adults. Some people expect their children to move out after graduating from high school while others expect their children to live with them until they get married (and still others expect to live together in a multigenerational household).

What further trips us up is that many times people don't know exactly what these values are or why they value certain things. We often internalize our family values and are unable to differentiate our own unique values from those of our families. Although Sara wanted to get her MBA and was accepted into a program at a good college, she has withdrawn twice from her enrolled courses. After some exploration, she realized that her reluctance came from growing up in a family that viewed corporations as greedy and materialistic. While this was never overtly stated to Sara, the message was still loud and clear. It came across in the way Sara's parents and grandparents exchanged looks of disapproval when they overheard investment bankers complaining about six-digit bonuses being too low, or during their discussions over the dinner table about the latest financial scandal. No wonder Sara couldn't get through business school. Before she could start addressing what was keeping her from her dreams, Sara had to become aware of this fundamental blockage rooted in conflicting values.

As I've described previously, there is potential for an extreme lack of separation between daughters and their mothers. As happens in other areas of a daughter's life, this issue of separation can cause confusion about whose values are whose. No two people share the exact same values. For instance, there may be an explicit family value that people are supposed to get married and have children. But a person may choose not share or act on their family's value. Sometimes the difference in a daughter's value may be threatening to her relationship with her mother. Annie shares her personal experience in this aspect: "My mom and I are close, but we don't necessarily understand each other. She's all about working hard, being thrifty. I didn't know how to tell her that I wanted to do something different. For someone who wants to focus on a writing career, I couldn't find the words to tell her." It was difficult for Annie to tell her mother about being a writer because it was easier not saying anything rather than making herself vulnerable. Deep down, she paradoxically wanted to be, and didn't want to be, separate from her mother. It is a common struggle for many adult daughters.

Personality

Personality traits are the combination of genetics ("nature") and environment ("nurture"). They are commonly known as character, persona or psyche, and are a building block that's hidden or less visible. It's not unusual for mothers to assume that their daughters will grow up to be similar to them. It circles back to separation. When a daughter's temperament is much different, though, her mother may view her as a difficult child; for instance, mothers with a subdued personality may be overly agitated by colicky or chatty baby daughters. Mothers who are more verbal and outgoing may feel rejected if their daughters are contemplative introverts. In general, it would benefit mothers (and fathers) to learn about personality theory in order to understand and accept their children's differences.

As an example of the confusion and misunderstanding resulting from personality differences, let's talk about Shelley and her mother, Kim. Kim was an intuitive person; she approached many facets of life from a big-picture or strategy-driven point of view. She created or identified ideas and possibilities but glossed over day-to-day minutiae. To Shelley's dismay, Kim couldn't understand why Shelley was so particular about coloring within the lines and why her checkbook had to be balanced down to the penny. Kim also never understood Shelley's heightened senses of sight, touch, and smells -- and how she pulled valuable information from these senses. These were the basis of Shelley's reality. She was far more sensitive to itchy tags on her clothes, strong perfumes, and how foods were prepared. Kim was less aware and could not focus on these details. This led to many misunderstandings between Kim and Shelley.

Without fully understanding personality theory, mothers may react to their daughters' differences with a "what's-wrong-with-you?" attitude instead of a fostering one. As a direct result, a daughter can develop insecurities, that erode self-esteem. How a mother handles these differences shapes a daughter's self-perception. There are high expectations for Copycat daughters to share similar personality traits with their mothers. A Maverick daughter works hard to disassociate herself in every aspect from her mother and is especially troubled when she realizes she is acting like her mother. It cannot be stressed how important it is for adult women to understand their personalities and accept themselves, as well as their similarities with and differences from, their mothers. When daughters embrace key aspects of themselves, and develop a supportive environment, they can move forward with satisfying careers.

It's different for male children primarily because they don't share a gender identity with their mothers. Mothers unconsciously view their female children as extensions of themselves and therefore may feel threatened when their daughters act or behave differently. Conversely, when daughters grow up and come into themselves, they may grow critical of their mothers for these differences. In our mother-daughter workshops, my mother and I saw many examples of women blaming their moms for not having showed them how to do something -- even if their mothers didn't have that particular experience, characteristic, or issue. The wish or push to become more like one another may be an ongoing issue for either woman (or both of them) in the mother-daughter relationship. My mother, Leah, took care of herself.

If we were at a cafe having tea and it was too cold, she never hesitated to ask one of the wait staff to warm it up. I see this as a good quality now, but it used to make me uncomfortable because it seemed as if she was "demanding". It's our lifelong process not only to understand ourselves but our mothers as well. These are two important reminders that I give to all women: don't beat yourself up for who you are, and don't beat up mom either.

Generations of women have a cause-and-effect impact on each other. Jacqueline is obsessive about arriving early for anything. She was always the first person at any scheduled meeting. Jacqueline's mother Elaine, on the other hand, was constantly late. It used to drive Jacqueline crazy. The pendulum can swing in opposite directions between the generations. We don't always think about the context of our behavior or the influence of previous generations, but this is how some personality traits and behaviors are passed down and formed. It follows us in a deep and cyclical manner, affecting us in ways we don't even think about, like Jacqueline and her punctuality.

Some kinds of work are better suited for certain personalities. Jane may find it energizing talking to different types of people; she'll enjoy a job where that element is a daily task. Leigh, however, prefers working independently and having minimal contact with people. She would not find Jane's job remotely ideal. When a woman is planning her career goals, she must consider these and other personality traits. Is it exciting exploring the unbeaten path or is her preference to follow more established routines? Is she cognizant of deadlines or does she believe that work should be submitted only when it has met quality standards? Does she lead by example or take charge?

There are countless and deep ways that our personalities interact with our work as well as the dynamics with our managers, colleagues, and clients. It is equally important to align our personality types with our careers. When this doesn't happen, it can make people very unhappy and cause problems at the office. There are lawyers who hate their work because it is adversarial, and they have an inherent aversion to fighting and conflict. When we look deeper into their personalities, we may discover that these lawyers are more "feelers" than "thinkers". Many of us may believe that we should make decisions only with objective facts. That's neither practical nor beneficial. We need to consider the interplay of our feelings in our decision-making process; to ignore it can lead to personality-career misalignment. Lilly was told her whole life by her mother that she could point out weaknesses in a person's argument like a shark could smell blood in the water. Lilly wanted to be a counselor, but she could only see herself the way her mother saw her. She thought she was too aggressive to go into counseling, a profession that secretly appealed to her. Lilly had to learn how to disregard her mother's views in favor of reframing her personality in her own voice so that she could pursue her career dreams. It was hard work, but eventually Lilly realized that her mother's opinions were just one aspect to consider, rather than the primary aspect.

Conclusion

Skills, interests, values, and personalities are all important and interrelated aspects of a person. Someone may be skilled with numbers but have no desire to work as an accountant. How do our personalities and values help to better identify the kind of career in which we would do well? We should start our career search out in the world only after we have conducted a thorough self-assessment through internal exploration. Whether it's looking for a new job online, considering going back to school, or talking to other people about options, our decision-making will become easier when we know our skills, interests, and personalities. When considered along with our understanding of how our unique mother-daughter dynamic may have affected our career choices, we have the best chance to move forward into a satisfying professional future.

Today, finding a career or job is not simply about providing potential employers with a list of one's experiences and skills. It's not about what a person has already accomplished; it's about her own personal brand. Employers are asking: What can you do that you haven't done before? Technology evolves quickly, so employers are less interested in the details of one's past on a resume. They're looking to understand who the potential employee is, what she is good at, and how she markets herself. They're looking for her electronic footprint. It's common practice for job applicants to articulate what they have to offer on social media and professional online networks. This is not easy work but instead requires abundant effort and faith in oneself. That's why it's important that we're aware of what could hold us back. If we are stuck in our mother's story of who we are and it leads us to pursue certain paths, we are not painting an accurate or sufficient picture of ourselves. To attain career satisfaction, we must take a leap of faith in ourselves and in our potential. We must put our strong message out there vividly -- with language, images, and rich possibilities -- through contemporary technologies and media. Sounds exhausting? It might be, but it's the kind of exhausting that exhilarates rather than drains. When women begin to understand that they are not repeats of their mothers (but also do not have to be opposites of her either), then they begin to understand that they are more than a sum of their past experiences.

In the next chapter, I'll delve into tips and solutions for women, regardless of their daughter types. In reading these tips and solutions, I encourage all women to think about the interplay between skills, values, personality, and interests. These building blocks are not independent of each other. They weave together in a complex, dynamic pattern that makes a woman who she is. When she is more fully aware of the different elements that might influence her professional pursuits, as well as how to utilize all of her strengths to realize those dreams, then she can unleash her full potential.

Chapter 9:

Tips and Solutions

I am struck that even in 2016, with all the knowledge that is available about career satisfaction, parents (with successful careers or not) continue to push their children toward careers without considering the children's unique skills, personality, and values. Instead, decisions are based on factors like financial stability, parents' own missed opportunities or failed dreams, and cultural or societal expectations. The tips and suggestions in this chapter are for grown-up women who now find themselves out of alignment with their careers. If something doesn't feel right about your present-day career choice, your job, and/or how you interact with authority, you may need a career check-up. It may have something to do with your mother-daughter dynamic. Paying attention to these tips will help you break free from the old strictures left over from this dynamic that may be holding you back in your career.

Standard career assessments not only help people identify their interests and skills, they also point people in the right direction. However, in order to address the kinds of issues that women may have identified from this book, the solutions and self-work needs to be deeper. They require more time and likely challenge assumptions a woman has made about herself and the world around her. Like a glacier, only a small tip of a person is visible. The rest of her, the heart of her, is hidden beneath the surface. Unearthing what makes her tick, and why, is not the type of work that can be accomplished in a short amount of time.

There are two basic reasons that introspection is difficult, especially for women who may not have spent any time focusing on, or uncovering, the hidden layers within themselves. First, change is hard and people naturally resist it. They fear the unknown; it provokes extreme anxiety. As bad as a situation might seem for a woman, there is some comfort in knowing what to expect, how others respond to her, and that she has an identity established from her current stable circumstances. When she changes her situation, she must work to re-establish herself, and that changes relationships with the people around her. She jumps off a metaphorical cliff, hoping that she will land on the ground safely.

Another reason introspection is hard work for many of us is because we are looking for reasons that have been concealed in the unconscious mind. As much as we remember our family, friends and teachers, as well as the paths we took to where we are today, we cannot discount our early, preconscious experiences, memories, and behaviors. These preconscious or unconscious elements determine a disproportionately large percentage of our decision-making. As I mentioned earlier, by six years old, we have already learned so much about the world, like what is scary or safe, how and whom to trust, and, what anger looks like. We barely remember how we learned these things but react according to these lessons every day. How can we consciously be more cognizant of these unconscious elements? One way is by paying closer attention to clues from our dreams and from our words and reactions that seem unreasonable. These unreasonable reactions probably signal a response that's coming from an unconscious emotion.

My approach to career counseling and career transition is deep. It takes work, dedication, and self-realization. Results will not happen overnight. Nonetheless, it is an effective method that works. The only way to fully address a person's career dissatisfaction in a holistic and comprehensive way is to fully explore her early relationships, particularly with her mother or primary caregiver. Using this lens and the tips below, she can start to build a new and more enriching career identity.

Tip #1: Learn Mom's Story

Hearing her mother's story is one of the most powerful solutions for a woman with career challenges. Most of us don't know more than our direct experiences with our mothers. While raising us, they might not have shared their stories because they were busy fulfilling their roles as the primary caregiver. Their stories are filled with beauty and pain, loss and gains, pride and disappointment, accomplishments and regrets, successes and failures. When we were children, it may not have been appropriate for our mothers to share their full stories. Nonetheless, that untold story holds the truth to why a daughter was raised in a certain way, what her mother passed on, and the legacy she leaves behind. Without knowing what her mom has gone through, a daughter can easily be judgmental and critical towards her. She may blame her mother for her own shortcomings or weaknesses, and feel angry with Mom about her own decisions. These negative emotions not only hinder the mother-daughter relationship; they also prevent an adult daughter from moving forward toward career satisfaction. However, by learning our mothers' stories, women will start to feel compassion for their mothers. Women may even begin to understand that their moms did the best they could with what they had or knew.

It may be hard to get a mom to open up; she may be reluctant to talk because she does not want to inflict her pain on her child, no matter what age her child may be now. Daughters, don't give up. Let her know that her story will help you to learn about yourself as well. More often than not, her maternal side will kick in, and she'll do what you so earnestly ask. It can also be incredibly therapeutic for her, too, and the two of you have a better chance to establish a deeper, more meaningful relationship. When a daughter expresses interest about her mother's life, it's amazing how the relationship dynamic can improve.

Note that this may not be true for some group of daughters who already know too much about their mothers' lives and woes. Bootstrap daughters had to take care of their mothers growing up and may feel resentful about the idea of learning more. This information helps adult daughters free themselves of the spoken and unspoken legacies their mothers left. If a woman's mother is no longer living, talk to different family members or friends about her. They each hold a different piece of her story or a side of her that a daughter may never have known. If a maternal grandmother is still available, women should ask her, too.

Sometimes women aren't quite sure what to ask. Here are some suggested questions to start the dialogue. Once mothers start to open up, women may find that they have a whole host of questions they have never thought to ask before!

- What was your relationship like with your own mother?
- In what ways did your mom support you?
- In what ways did you wish your mom could have supported you more?
- What kind of career or work options did you feel were open to you?
- How did you feel about your work at home or in the work place? Are, or were you, happy with them?
- What would you do differently?
- What are, or were, your hopes and dreams for me?
- One thing I want to understand more about in your life is _____ (fill in the blank)

Tip #2: People Tell Stories That They Themselves Need To Hear

Mark Savickas is a brilliant career theorist and educator who developed career construction theory. This theory focuses on helping clients "pattern the past" with a narrative approach to help people find purpose, meaning and usefulness in their lives. Exploring early recollections in childhood, role models, heroes and stories all help reveal a vocational personality. Exploring mother-daughter themes through the tool of storytelling is a rich and meaningful way to access important themes that permeate throughout our lives. These stories give important clues and are a window into who we are and how we may, or may not, be satisfied in the world. As women tell their own life stories, I encourage them not to block out memories or experiences that are insignificant, traumatic, or positive. All of our experiences contribute to who we become. When a woman understands the themes in her life story, particularly the pain, this can help her glean insight into the parts of herself that need to heal. This healing often manifests itself in her life work, which is a deep, important, and effective way of healing. For example, American actress, Ashley Judd, writes in her memoir that she was often alone and lonely while her mother, Naomi, and sister, Wynonna, pursued their singing careers. Now she spends her spare time as a political activist helping the voiceless to have a voice. Her life is built around the idea of support and community. A trauma in early childhood may generate an important theme for people to work out and work through in their lives and careers. By helping people become conscious of this, I can help them identify important themes and meaning for their work.

Tip #3: Get a Role Model or Surrogate

When I was gathering information for this book, I asked women to give one piece of advice for other women struggling with career transition. The number one answer was to get a role model. This was said to me over and over in many different ways: *"Look for someone else to fill the role"*; *"Find a mentor or confidante"*; *"Ask for advice from a boss or older colleague"*; one woman even told me she was looking for surrogate parents in all of her jobs! Others tell me they are looking for someone who could "show me myself" because their mothers only showed them whom she wanted them to be. The power of a role model is enormous for women. My clients whose mothers were not role models are struck at the mere question: "Who were your role models?" It doesn't occur to them that people have an easier time doing something because they have been able to watch and learn from their mentors.

We are at a pivotal time in history. In the United States, there are many women who are 50 or older whose mothers grew up in eras where women had scant or no job prospects. Even women growing up in the 1970s, were still being told that their main career choices were teacher, nurse, or secretary. Though career options have expanded dramatically for us today, we still don't have the same opportunities as men, and, we often have to consider compromising or stalling our careers in order to be the primary caregivers for our children. In a *Ted Talk,* Facebook COO, Sheryl Sandberg, said the following: "Women are not making it to the top of any profession anywhere in the world...[of]190 heads of state, nine are women... In the corporate sector, women at the top (C-level jobs, board seats) tops out at 15%, 16%... We also have another problem, which is that women face harder choices between professional success and personal fulfillment."

Sheryl Sandberg's astute observation results from slow-to-evolve views of women in the workplace. We don't have the opportunities because our mothers didn't. Despite women's incredible progress in the workplace over the last 50 years, many women still struggle without the support of a role model whom they can identify with, and, to a certain degree, emulate. It makes a remarkable difference in workplace challenges, when our mothers are our guides. For those daughters whose mothers could not fulfill this role, it may be relatively easy to identify potential mentors. Although they may imagine it needs to be someone in a powerful position at their companies, it does not. Nor do they need to have a formal mentoring program in place to build a mentorship. A successful mentor-mentee relationship requires women on both sides to be able to see elements of themselves in the other. In some ways, we are looking for a maternal figure (sometimes literally) and it's also not unusual to conjure up images of women with major influence over our lives. That's also not always the case. In the examples below, there are no traditional role models; women should keep their minds open as they look for one to guide them in their careers.

Pree is a Bootstrap daughter with an immigrant mother and works in an office for a woman named Val. At work, Pree takes the time to figure things out on her own, just like she did when she was growing up. From a young age, she was the translator for her parents and completed many of their legal documents. Although Pree thinks highly of her boss, she has never named Val as one of her role models. It simply never occurred to Pree. After further discussion and self-introspection, though, she realized how much she enjoyed learning from Val, primarily because Val takes the time to explain every step of the process and the reasoning behind her approach. It's clear to Pree that Val is interested in not just showing her how to do specific things, but in really passing on the knowledge. At almost every annual performance review meeting that Pree has with Val, Pree has an emotional reaction during the meeting and wonders why. It takes Pree some time before she realizes that those emotional reactions denote subconscious recognition that Val's guidance is a relatively new kind of maternal teaching that Pree didn't have during her childhood. While it makes her feel uncomfortable, she also acknowledges that it is wonderful to be able to allow new maternal figures to "parent" her. Pree doesn't have to hold onto patterns of the past. By fully embracing and recognizing Val's mentorship, Pree has grown tremendously.

Cynthia, a 49-year old emergency room doctor in Dallas, had to understand how to succeed in medicine on her own. Her mother was a stay-at-home mom who occasionally dabbled in art. While Cynthia has no trouble making decisions in her field of practice, she can be plagued with self-doubt about accomplishing other goals. She is keenly aware that men in general act more confidently and take more risks than she does. This is true for many professions. Men are more likely to apply for jobs where they may only meet 60% of the required qualifications. Women, on the other hand, generally do not apply to positions unless they believe they meet 100% of the qualifications. When Cynthia entered the medical profession more than 20 years ago, she was the only female doctor on staff. To succeed, she had to learn how to push past her insecurities to do all kinds of things she never thought she could do. Sometimes, she felt like "a fraud". This scared her tremendously (and is a common theme with my clients). Because she didn't have a real role model for work, Cynthia created one in her head. While she "winged" it and there were occasional mishaps, the female doctors who started their careers after Cynthia now look to her for guidance about how to combine raising a family and climbing the career ladder as well as Cynthia did. Cynthia is beginning to embrace this role because she realizes that she can pass on important knowledge to future generations of women doctors.

Role models come in all shapes and sizes. Like Pree, some women may already have a role model and not even know it. Or, like Cynthia, others may have had to create one. It's time to expand the definition of what makes a role model. I tell my clients to consider the following questions:

- What attributes does the mentor have that are admirable?
- What do you wish your mother could have told or showed you about your career?
- What aspects of this mentor's career do you wish to emulate?

Tip #4: Break the Isolation

Many women believe that they are the only people who are experiencing career challenges. Their friends, colleagues, and peers seem to possess an astounding level of self-assurance. They wonder how these wonder women can possibly do it all and have it all. Here's a little secret: as accomplished and as successful as these other women are, they may have just as many self-doubts and insecurities as you do. And here's the kicker -- when they look at you, they're wondering how you can seem so together! The takeaway is that women are not alone in feeling doubts. Many of us have gone through periods in our careers where we felt lost, confused, unhappy, or uncertain. When women realize just how normal it is to feel this way and start to vocalize these feelings, they may find that there are many people who can empathize, including their partners, family, friends, or others, outside of their immediate social circle. You only need to reach out and talk about it openly.

Tip #5: Challenge Your Current Situation

Although many of us may be unhappy with our current work situations, we don't necessarily change them for a variety of reasons. When the situation at work is only mildly uncomfortable instead of severe, many of us intentionally choose to remain where we are. The following questions prevent us from exploring the unknown:

- If I switch careers, will I be able to live and spend in the manner to which I'm accustomed?
- Will I have to start at the bottom again?
- What if I'm not successful?

Essentially, while these questions are valid, the fear behind them may not be. To combat unfounded fears, a woman must first probe what's really holding her back. Could she hesitate to move in a new or different direction because she's afraid? Once a person recognizes the presence of fear, she can see how to work through the challenges and blockages to a more satisfying career. She can begin to acknowledge that change is difficult, and that she may need to overcome unanticipated barriers linked to change. She can also realize that despite these difficulties, plenty of other people have been where she is and yet successfully transition into their dream careers every day. I should know. Throughout my 25 years as a career counselor, I have helped and witnessed hundreds of clients tackle and overcome career change.

Take Esperanza, for example. She worked in finance for five years and, while she was unsatisfied with her work, she didn't know what she wanted to do instead. We spoke on a weekly basis for about a year before she decided to quit her job and apply to art school. Initially, the process was daunting; the art school application required an art portfolio, something she had never created. She did it anyway and was accepted into her school of choice. Five years later, she can barely recognize herself in the person she used to be. Today, she looks forward to getting up every morning so that she can design logos for t-shirts sold online to stores and people around the world. I tell women to try to remember a time in their lives when they felt happier and successful. What were they doing? Can they challenge their current situations to get there again?

Tip #6: TRUST Yourself

No one knows a woman better than herself. She knows what she likes and doesn't like. Tucked away within her, she also knows what kind of work would make her happier. I encourage women considering a change to reach back into those memories of what made them happy and explore the career potential in those areas.

When I administer career assessments to my clients, they often reflect on how interesting it is to see the results in a structured way. They also find it helpful to review or confirm what makes them tick in the framework of that assessment. They comment on how they thought about a particular career or industry repeatedly in the past. The assessment is very affirming but not the most useful part of the career counseling process. Many people are already intrinsically aware of what work makes them happy. They simply need to lower the volume of static that distracts them from their true career desires. When they can't do it themselves, for whatever reason, that's when it's time to seek a career counselor. The counselor's job is to affirm a woman's true and realistic career aspirations, to set goals, and to help guide her into taking action to meet those goals. It sounds simple, to trust one's own instincts, but it's not. Seen through the lens of the mother-daughter dynamic, a woman may have a difficult time separating the ghost of her mother's voice from her own. Without objective guidance, it may not be possible for someone to be able to recognize her own needs and desires from her mother's.

Tip #7: Separate From Mother

People used to ask me and my mother about our relationship all the time. They correctly assumed that we were close in order to be able to conduct workshops about the mother-daughter relationship. They often wanted to know what a healthy mother-daughter relationship looked like, and how my mom and I were able to accomplish that. As I used to tell women, every mother-daughter relationship is unique. Every relationship uses and requires different elements for establishing a healthy dynamic. However, there are some commonalities.

In a healthy mother-daughter relationship, each woman respects the other. While they share information, they may not necessarily share every aspect of their lives. There are healthy boundaries so that a mother and her daughter can grow in separate directions. If a mother and her daughter are too close, adult daughters are sometimes hindered from moving forward in life. Daughters may appear to be moving ahead in their careers, for example, physically moving away, or taking a job that offers more money or responsibilities. However, both mother and daughter may regard this as a betrayal towards the mother, especially if it results in her daughter focusing on something or someone else, or if the mom disapproves of her daughter's choices. True separation between mother and daughter is psychological and emotional more than it is physical. A physical separation alone does not necessarily allow a woman to explore her wishes and realities that may be different from her mother's. I had a client who moved all the way to Alaska to get away from her "mother's clutches". Others would cut off all contact with their moms in an attempt to be "their own women". Still others were literally waiting for their mothers to die before choosing a satisfying career! It shouldn't surprise anyone reading this book this, that none of these acts actually helped the adult daughters separate from their mothers. All of these extreme acts of separation were superficial and therefore illusory. The daughters were unable to break free from the constraints of being too in sync with their mothers, and thus remained in unhappy jobs and relationships longer than necessary. Some adult daughters have spent years in therapy over this particular topic. Given the deep and intense connection in the relationship, separation issues can be very intense. At this point, you might be asking how a woman can tell if she's too close with her mom. First, it's important to identify the problem. Is one person in the mother-daughter relationship overly dependent on, or overly protective of, the other? Or, does there seem to be an imbalance when it comes to concern and attentiveness? These are all signs that a healthy separation has not yet been achieved. An adult daughter who is overly dependent on her mother's opinions needs to discover who she is, separate from her mother. I ask women to ponder the following: think about the interests you may have always wanted to explore that your mom doesn't find even remotely fascinating. I encourage an adult daughter to delve into these subject areas. Perhaps she should make new friends and begin to share information with her mother on an as-needed basis. Her mother may naturally resist this change; ultimately, though, she will see it is healthy for the relationship. Early in life, we need a symbiotic relationship with our mothers. We depend on her for sustenance, safety, and unconditional love. As an adult, while we still depend on her, we also need to differentiate ourselves from her. The result should be two separate women, each with her own strengths and limitations, who accept the similarities and differences in one another.

It's important to point out that separation is a lifelong process and not a one-time event. It can take years for women to create the healthy boundaries that prevent them from feeling the "sting" of their mothers' judgments and criticisms. However, once a healthy degree of separation occurs, women can truly begin to see who they are, what they like, and in which direction to move. Finally, note that separation is not about ignoring one's mom. It is possible for women to be emotionally separate from their mothers and still be close with them. It may mean that while your mother wanted you to be a lawyer, and you chose to go into acting, it's healthy for Mom to be concerned about the financial stability of your choices but, nonetheless, she should support your decisions and encourage you to pursue your goals.

When their daughters are still fetuses in their wombs, mothers have expectations of who their daughters will become. This is true for all types of daughters, be they Ivies, Mavericks, Butterflies, Copycats, or Bootstraps. How a mother expresses these expectations will differ, but one principle remains the same: daughters do not like disappointing their mothers. It is a burden for daughters to believe that they are expected to please their mothers all the time, especially when you consider that this is an impossible task. You cannot always please another person all the time. Many daughters are very concerned that they will be rejected or unloved if they don't fulfill their mothers' expectations for them. When a daughter learns how to separate from her mother, her mother's disapprovals don't carry the same weight. She has developed enough awareness of her mother's limitations as well as the self-awareness to pursue her own goals anyway.

Tip #8: Heal Relationship With Mom

If an adult daughter's relationship with Mom is troubled or conflicted, there is no simple, quick fix-all solution. I am not going to attempt to cover such a complex topic in this book, but I will say that when women work on healing this relationship, it helps in many aspects of their

121

lives, including career. I can also offer the following recommendations on what women should START doing, STOP doing and CONTINUE doing with their moms. Though it doesn't happen overnight, the demands and relationships at work will seem less stressful. In order to feel good about oneself as a woman, one must first reconcile this critical primal relationship. Reconciliation is also important even if one's mother is deceased. The power of mother can still hold enormous weight.

When it comes to Mom, <u>START</u> doing the following:
- Communicating better and more deeply
- Being more honest
- Being more nurturing
- Feeling more loving and less angry
- Being more of a daughter and less of a friend
- Being more confident despite any anxieties coming from Mom
- Spending time more on your terms
- Working on accepting Mom and hoping that she starts accepting you!

When it comes to Mom, <u>STOP</u> doing the following:
- Being so protective of her
- Feeling anxious about not being perfect in her eyes
- Feeling guilty about either not spending enough time with her or giving her enough
- Telling her what to do and how to do it (without being asked for an opinion)
- Being judgmental

When it comes to Mom, <u>CONTINUE</u> doing the following:
- Feeling okay about being separate and different
- Spending quality time together to get to know one another
- Learning to grow, separately and together

<u>**Tip #9**</u>: Assess Your Career Profile

A powerful way for women to discover their true selves is through career assessment. These assessments can help women gain insights about many things such as interests, skills, achievements, knowledge, learning style, personality, attitudes, and values. Assessments can also be helpful with decision-making. If you're unclear in any aspect I've mentioned, I highly encourage you to add career assessment as a valuable tool. I could write a whole book highlighting individual ones. Needless to say, there are many kinds of assessments available. *The National Career Development Association* ("NCDA") is a great resource for comprehensive overviews of the different career assessments. You can find more information on their website, <u>www.ncda.org</u>.

<u>**Tip #10**</u>: Prepare for Interviews

The emotional wounds formed in childhood, and carried into adulthood, can sabotage our efforts when we present ourselves for a new job. It's even tougher when we're not even conscious that we are carrying these emotional wounds or cognizant of how they formed. These early childhood imprints stay with us, and inconveniently surface at the most inopportune times. Below is a list of things women have told me that illustrate the pain and issues that continue to dominate and curtail their professional lives, particularly during job interviews:

- "I should've worn a new suit. I bet I didn't make the best impression. My mother wanted to take me shopping, but there are always strings attached."
- "I know the hiring manager liked me, I always know how to make a good first impression with men. My mother definitely taught me those skills."
- "Mom tells me I'm like a dog with a bone; I should've just dropped that last point I was trying to make, but the interviewer just made me SO angry!"
- "I never know how to answer questions about technical skills. I feel like it's important, but my

123

mother wasn't any good at computers and she's always saying I'm just like her. Instead of admitting or denying anything, I usually end up evading the question. Is that bad?"

- "Ever since I was diagnosed with bipolar disorder, my mom won't stop worrying about me. I know this means I probably can't have a satisfying work life, but a part of me feels like I'm smart enough to try anyway."
- "Why do I assume nobody will hire me and if they do, I will just feel like a fraud?"

This negative thinking does not have to hold you back on your interviews. It is so important to prepare for an interview by understanding stories of the past that have made you successful and how they relate to future opportunities, including your best strengths that you will be bringing into the workplace and all of your positive qualities that you're trying to sell. Too many times, we walk into an interview thinking about what we're trying to hide from the interviewer– including gaps of employment, academic failures, terminations and insecurities. Instead, think about how you can connect with the interviewer and show him/her your best self. It takes practice but when you bring your self-confidence with you to the interview, the sky is the limit and you can then assess whether you have the right fit for a new job.

Tip #11: Challenge Your Choices

Upon my first encounter with clients, it's not uncommon for them to either tell me that they don't know which path to choose or that they feel empty in their jobs or careers. Before I begin any assessment or delve further into the counseling process, I always ask my clients about their upbringing, the choices they have made, and their history covering education, family life, medical conditions, and work. Some women struggle tremendously with making decisions. By now, I hope it's clear how much a person's childhood impacts her future choices; this includes how her parents dealt with learning differences, academic successes or failures, and the decision-making process in general. When I help clients look at early childhood choices of hobbies, interests, and extracurricular activities, they always reveal relevant patterns for today's career dilemma. Kids know what they like and what they don't like. They're also not afraid to own it. As adults, *if* we can identify what we like and are interested in, then it gives us a clearer picture about the line of work we should be pursuing.

But I find that the most difficult question for adults is one question that most children easily answer: "What do you like?" Although kids can readily rattle off a list, most adults answer, "What do you mean?" That's sad to me because somewhere along the way grown-ups lose sight of their interests, while self-doubt and insecurity settle in. "If I don't spend at least five hours per week doing this activity, then it means it's not really a hobby or interest" pops up multiple times throughout sessions with my clients. Or, "I know so many people that are better informed than I am about sailing, so I can't really say it's a real interest of mine." Why do we do this to ourselves? If we spend any time doing something, reading about it, talking to our friends about it, then, it's an interest! Of course, career choice is not that simple, and includes many more complex factors, including other aspects of a person like her skills, personality and values. However, I tell my clients to go back through their childhood choices. Is there a pattern in what she liked?

Another exercise that I use with my clients is to have them think back to a big decision they made in their past. It could be about the majors they studied in school, the pastimes they kept or dropped, a college they attended, or a job offer. Next, I tell them to try to figure out why they made the decision that they did. What I'm hoping women will see is that their true interests are not a secret, and, as helpful as a career assessment may be, it won't reveal suddenly and surprisingly what they like. Instead, it will be more of an "ah-hah!" moment. These interests were there all along, but were not noticed because of the noise of external factors. Here are just a few distracting static sounds I've heard about from women, but this list could be pages long:

- "I always liked writing, but gave it up when my mother embarrassed me by reading my work in front of her friends."
- "I was always drawing and painting, but I was told that art isn't a serious career choice, and, that I'd never be able to support myself. Since the message that I should never depend on a man for money was also drilled into me, I knew I needed to choose something stable."
- "When given a choice, I'm always outside. While I love moving, breathing in fresh air, and being in touch with nature and animals, I was told that kind of thing was for lumberjacks and other blue collar workers, and I was too smart to waste my brains on that sort of thing."
- "I love to travel and meet new people, and I've always wanted a career in that industry. But everyone in my immediate family is a doctor or lawyer, and I didn't pursue hospitality management because I felt it wasn't prestigious enough."
- "I was always playing therapist when I was a child, like Lucy to Charlie Brown in the Peanuts comic strips. But my mom was being physically abused by my dad. I never thought I could really help people if I couldn't save my own mother from those awful beatings."

These examples highlight negative thinking, and I could fill pages with all the positive thinking as well. We tend to put more credence on the negative thoughts and let them interfere. By searching for the positive decisions and stories in a woman's life, woman can see how they can repeat success. Challenge the problematic choices but celebrate the positive ones! We all have both.

Tip #12: Allow Room for Mistakes

There is a great quote from the Baal Shem Tov, *"Never ask the way from someone who knows, because then you can never get lost."* There are many people who choose a career path at a young age and try very hard to stay on that path. But life gets in the way. Very few people have a career that follows a straight line because people or opportunities propel us in new and different directions. What is the consequence of not getting lost? Or, a better question is -- what are the benefits of getting lost? You learn to trust your instincts, and you gain confidence from knowing you can find your way. Most importantly, you learn to stop fearing the risks of taking a different path in life or of not finding your way. Getting lost is a good thing. Life doesn't happen on a linear line, no matter how hard people may try to make it so. If women can learn to let go and accept the tangential paths that they will inevitably take in life, they will learn that mistakes are part of the process and ultimately can provide profound lessons for their careers and lives.

Tip #13: Surrender to Go Deeper

It's hard to give up our notion of ourselves that we took a lifetime to develop and "perfect". We tell ourselves stories about who we are, what we do, why we stay in a problematic job, and why we're stuck. But when we try to let go of that story we created and we challenge it, great things will happen. When we try to hold a new or difficult pose in yoga, our bodies wish to revert back to the natural state. Continued practice makes it easier to stretch into new dimensions and literally change our bodies and our minds. It's about surrendering what was, in order to come up with something new. When you surrender what you are holding on to, you can let go of the stories that you create in your head that prevent you from moving forward. This relates to career because we can't always be defined by parents' messages of past negative work experiences. We have to be defined by who we are, challenge those assumptions, and create new pathways. Women will dig deeper into themselves and discover new ways of thinking and being. As a matter of fact, neuroscientists tell us that we can actually create new patterns and realities in the brain by allowing ourselves to experience the world differently. Mindfulness practices like yoga and meditation can help us do this physically which helps us get there emotionally.

Tip #14: Be Mindful of the Cultural Minefields

It's important to note that certain cultures have power differentials between genders. Those power differentials can play into the mother-daughter dynamic. In some cultures, women are more deferential to men while in others, women hold more power, especially if they are single parents. In cultures and societies where women are more or less revered, it's very tough for first generation daughters to parse out how their mothers are seen through a cultural lens. From a young age, girls are watching to learn which gender has the power in the home and in society. Cultural norms are embedded in their mothers' decisions. If a daughter is a first generation or second generation American, there is an added layer of confusion, pressure, role modeling, or expectation if her mother was born in a significantly different culture or time. Understanding this phenomenon can help women blame their moms less for not being able to be role models and to not judge themselves too harshly for making different choices.

Tip #15: Revisit the Tips!

Revisit the tips in the daughter chapters as well as the ones in this chapter. If at first you don't succeed, revisit and try again. Sometimes readiness and timing are significant factors when it comes to making change. A tip or suggestion that might not have been helpful days or weeks ago might have new appeal.

Chapter 10:

Daughter Type and Leadership

Leadership is such a critical issue in the workplace that no book would be complete without exploring the leadership through the lens of the mother-daughter dynamic and the daughters model. I've seen how the frameworks apply towards leadership, both in my private practice and as a human resources executive. There are two angles to explore. First, what are the potential strengths and limitations of each daughter's leadership styles? Second, how do we respond to leaders of a particular style?

The Ivy Daughter as a Leader

Generally speaking, an Ivy daughter is not afraid to lead. She likes the power and has the potential to be a strong leader. The concern with an Ivy leader is that she might like her power too much. If she has unfulfilled needs, she can become a micromanager. She might also look to her staff to meet her own emotional needs; for example, inviting them or herself to evening dinners, asking or telling overly personal information, and establishing unhealthy boundaries. Her team may feel like they have to tiptoe, walk on eggshells, or "feed" her need for connection in order to be successful. She may be sensitive to rejection or indifference, making it tricky for her employees to navigate through her moods or expectations.

If an Ivy daughter's energy is channeled constructively and she is aware of her tendencies, she can be a strong and powerful advocate for her team. She'll see them as an extension of herself, taking up their causes at work. But if she has problematic relationships across the organization, her team members may fear this will extend to them and so they'll be careful to keep their distance from her. This perpetuates the Ivy daughter's feelings of rejection. If, however, her employees understand or empathize with the Ivy leader, they can develop compassion for her style rather than feeling angry, if she is overly controlling or micromanaging. There is considerable potential for a great team with a close bond to form. Bear in mind, though, that each team member's response will be triggered at work by her own history, which includes her daughtering type and mother-daughter dynamic. Healthy relationships at work require a delicate balance among team members, and each person's awareness of what she brings into the workplace. For example, Maverick daughters will likely have trouble getting along with an Ivy leader because they're still seeking freedom (in their hearts) from a controlling mother. They will not be able to tolerate an Ivy manager whose power seems too great. Ivy leaders must learn to get along with a variety of employees or they will not be as effective in a leadership role.

The Maverick Daughter as a Leader

Women of this daughter type are sensitive about not being too controlling with their employees. Their sensitivities come from their own restrictive experiences. They may lead by example and allow their team to find their own way. Even if Maverick daughters in leadership positions may still be rebelling in their relationships with their own bosses, their management style is more open and flexible with subordinates. Many adult Maverick daughters are still finding themselves. That means they may move onto the next job or career before they can really leave their mark, however much their team appreciates their spirit. Maverick daughters may not be in it for the long haul, as they are still seeking their own career identities. Sometimes a great job or supervisor creates an environment where Mavericks choose to stay longer than anticipated, but this will vary from woman to woman. Employees reporting up to a Maverick daughter typically will not feel her rebelliousness; Maverick daughters' buttons may get pushed by employees who are too controlling or critical or have other traits which remind her of her mother. While Mavericks can be pleasant bosses, they may not, or cannot be, reliable mentors while working through their own challenges.

The Butterfly Daughter as a Leader

Butterfly daughters may make wonderful role models and mentors, generally giving other women the career guidance and support that they might not have had otherwise. They may suffer from imposter syndrome, wondering if they deserve to be in their executive level roles; as a result, they may initially feel insecure about being leaders. Butterfly daughters may not aspire to higher positions because of their insecurities, which can create self-imposed glass ceilings. With time and with each accomplishment, however, Butterfly daughters' self-confidence will grow. In turn, they may mentor and promote employees from underrepresented groups. Recognition and acknowledgement go a long way for Butterfly daughters who are leaders. They will need to understand that they are doing a good job and if they need help with leadership skills, they should seek out coaches to show them how. A Butterfly daughter may have reservations about what she considers "a man's world". I strongly recommend women's leadership initiatives, support networks, and other training opportunities.

The Copycat Daughter as a Leader

Because Mom was a role model from the very start, Copycat daughters are likely to be confident leaders. When she feels she lacks some skill, the Copycat may seek out mentors at work; after all, she is used to close female relationships (as she had one with her mom) and values that at work. She will get tapped for leadership roles as she projects confidence in the workplace, even if she has her private insecurities. Copycat leaders have to remind themselves that not every woman is a Copycat. Other women may need more direction and confidence to move forward. Copycat daughters may be very focused on upward mobility at work. They may not let things (or people) stand in their way of advancement. Depending on her personality and role, such an adult daughter may be tough or easy, demanding or laid back. She knows how to play in the sandbox and knows what it takes to get ahead in a man's, or a woman's, world. If a Copycat daughter emulated a mother who was not a strong leader, she may identify with that limitation as well.

The Bootstrap Daughter as a Leader

Bootstrap daughters may make solid leaders, since they are used to being the "grown up" at home their whole lives. From a very young age, they made household decisions, had to be the voice (and voice of reason) for family members, and carried on their shoulders a heavy weight that allowed the family to function. Leadership generally comes very naturally to these women. Though they have their insecurities, they generally do not reveal them to subordinates. Bootstrap leaders must be careful about taking on too much work. I remind my Bootstrap clients that they no longer have the weight of the world on their shoulders, even if they feel like they still do.

Bootstrap daughters may make demanding leaders. They expect other employees to provide the same high-quality work as they may put out themselves, so, Bootstrap daughters should be mindful of different daughter types, especially women who are Ivies. They may be impatient and unable to empathize with, Ivy daughters. As one Bootstrap daughter put it: "Hey, I had a difficult childhood, too. You don't see me throwing a pity party." Bootstrap leaders had to learn how to communicate at a young age. For whatever reason, they were the parentified daughter and had to become very tuned in to people. Many can read a room with laser-beam accuracy and respond shrewdly. Though they may believe they need to better manage conflict, many exude a calm and confident style during difficult situations.

Conclusion

Leaders come in many shapes and sizes. For every daughter leader type, there are infinite variations on these themes and leadership styles. Of course, each work situation varies. But one's daughter type definitely extends into career choice, career development, workplace dynamics, and leadership style. This summary presents just the tip of the iceberg to get adult daughters thinking and exploring their leadership types from a daughtering perspective. As women think about their career challenges, I hope that they will use this framework in their interactions with others to foster resolution, change, or at the very least, peace of mind.

Chapter 11:

A Guide for Raising Your Own Daughters

If you have a young daughter, you've probably had moments when you marvel at the myriad choices and opportunities she'll have for a career. Amid all the possibilities, it's not unusual for mothers to worry about whether a daughter will make the "right" choices that will lead her onto a happy, fulfilling path, personally and professionally.

You may wonder if she's going to have the same dreams as you, if she's going to choose the same career, or make the same choices. You may hope that she'll have more opportunities for success than you did. You also hope that when she's grown, she'll carry a part of you with her. I tell women all the time that their stories are (at times, unavoidably) bonded with their mom's life experiences. The truth is, your daughter will make choices with which you'll agree, and also choices that will make you proud, disappointed, worried, angry, and happy, as well as a whole gamut of emotions in-between. She'll go through a period where she hangs on to your every word and move. Then, almost too quickly, she'll ignore your seemingly practical or simple advice for no apparent reason. Your relationship with your daughter will define her, just as I hope you've learned by now how much your own relationship with your mom defines you.

How can you be the most constructive in preparing her for a satisfying work life? Here are ten practical tips, gleaned from my decades of experience, that will support your daughter so that she can enjoy a fulfilling career with minimal drama and difficulties.

Ten Important Ways to Encourage Your Daughter's Career Choices

1. **Allow your daughter room for error.** Of course, you should definitely step in if she is going to do something unsafe or harmful. Context matters in this tip. As a parent, your first priority is to keep her safe. But a young daughter can learn from the value of "natural consequences". If your daughter doesn't do her homework, let her fail! (Perhaps easier said than done, but it is worthwhile to consider).

2. **Let her explore her interests.** Studies have shown that people with careers that are aligned with their interests are happier. Even if it doesn't appeal to you, let your daughter take up a hobby of her choosing. If she has a choice of math or art for a summer program, start a two-way dialogue with her about what she'd like to learn.

3. **Don't impose your values on her.** I am not speaking about core religious or ethical values. Your daughter is not an extension of yourself. That means she'll probably find that some things that are important to you, are not as important to her. For example, if you work in a bank and value financial security, your daughter may end up being a writer, a career that has less stability. That's okay. No matter how different she may be from you, she'll still love you and need your support.

4. **Don't pressure her to settle down before she is ready!** The years between 18 and 26 are prime-time for women's career development. During this period, young women are exploring their professional interests, testing out their theories, and identifying their strengths and where they attain true satisfaction. Today, women don't have to get married right out of school; there is plenty of time to meet a

partner and/or have children at a later age, if they so choose.

5. **Let her be a child to the extent that she can.** "Susie's so dependable, she's like a miniature grown up!" If your daughter is helping you run the household or taking care of family members, does she have time to play? Or to make believe and be just plain silly? If the answer is no, then find ways to free up her time and fewer responsibilities. She'll have plenty of years ahead of her to be a grownup; give her the opportunity now to be carefree and to explore herself. Otherwise, she may grow up unaware of her true interests, which could lead to less satisfaction with her career choices.

6. **Don't expect her to fulfill your unfulfilled dreams.** Perhaps you gave up becoming a musician because you had to go into the family business. Perhaps you didn't have time to focus on your work because you focused on your family life. Whatever your unfulfilled dreams, and the reasons they are unfulfilled, your daughter shouldn't be expected to live them out on your behalf. She is entitled to tune into her own desires but might not notice them if yours are stuck in her head.

7. **Remember that her separation is not a rejection!** There will come a time when your daughter rejects your advice and branches out of your comfort zone. This generally happens during adolescence and, although her withdrawal may be painful, it signifies normal progression into healthy adulthood. The more you try to make her feel like this is unnatural and abnormal, the unhealthier the separation will become. Although separation is normal, it's a big issue for both of you. Be mindful of it and let go to a reasonable extent if you find yourself holding onto your daughters too tightly. If you're not sure you're holding on too tightly, here's a red-flag example I often hear from parents: "We have to work on this essay and fill

out these college applications before the deadlines." No, *we* don't, *she* does!

8. **Be her mirror, show her strengths.** Sometimes the teachers and grading standards in our educational system don't allow our daughters to shine or see their best selves. Your daughter might be a creative thinker who may be boxed in by a rigid teacher. For example, there is the classic case of children scolded in class for drawing a purple cow. It's your job to make a daughter aware of her strengths.

9. **Create opportunities.** Your daughter may be free to make her own choices, but that doesn't mean you shouldn't offer your advice. Be her advocate. Make sure she understands the pros and cons of her decisions. Point out opportunities whenever they arise and let her decide what she wants to do with those opportunities. Trust me, in the long run she'll appreciate it and thank you for being there.

10. **Get your own life and career together!** The greatest gift you can give your daughter is being her role model. Show her that it's never too late to get a degree or to switch jobs and careers. Whether or not it seems noticeable, she is watching you closely. Her chances to succeed in life are significantly higher when she's seen you do it.

Of course, when it comes to raising children, there's no perfect solution, and there probably will be some compromises along the way. But if you understand who you and your daughter are, what makes both of you tick, where you excel and what's important, you can begin to make solid decisions based on who you are and who she is, and what both of you want to pursue. When you've achieved this goal, you will not only find a better path in life, but you may also be able to connect, or empathize with, your daughter in ways you never thought possible.

After reading these ten tips on how to nurture your daughter's career, you may realize that you, your daughter, and your mother are different daughter types. Behaviors of one generation cause reactions in the next that in turn affect future generations. I had a client whose mother owned a small business that kept her away from home during her daughter's childhood. When her daughter grew up, she chose not to be like her mother and stayed home to raise her own children, even though she was conflicted about not pursuing a career. It wouldn't surprise me if her daughters grow up choosing something different than their mother and seeking other role models in their professions of choice. There's no such thing as a perfect mother, and there's no perfect answer to life's issues. It's okay, if our daughters are different from us, just like it's okay for us to be different from our mothers. What we want for our daughters is for them to be the best of whom they are. To do that, we all should provide as much healthy parenting as we can -- in raising our children and in supporting their skills, interests, and values so that they move into their chosen careers with the best foot forward.

Conclusion

Ultimately, the keys to a good life are finding purpose, joy, and passion. When people are unable to make a keenly desired career choice, they lose the chance to have this key. When they are reminded how they were motivated in the past, they might just be able to find that energy to do it again. Part of my job is to help people see the gratifying possibilities that unfold when people take risks and make changes -- they could be happier and more successful as a result. I don't discount how hard change is. I know that change is scary and unfamiliar. Most people change for two reasons: to avoid pain (i.e., running away from something); or, to move toward pleasure (i.e., running to something). If you're yearning for change but haven't done anything about it yet, remind yourself WHY you're seeking something new. Start with small steps. We spend so much time in pursuit of work, that it's critical for our work to be enriching and satisfying. Many people believe they don't have the time or resources to make life-changing decisions. Or they say that they're past the age of change. They hold themselves back and wind up unhappy.

When women start talking about their mothers, what their relationships were like and how their mothers influenced their lives, you can't stop the conversation. That's what happened for the twelve years, from 1990 through 2003, when my mother and I ran workshops for mothers and their adult daughters. The courses sold out every single time. Each workshop was more powerful and intense than the previous one. Daughters invited their mothers, mothers invited their daughters, and mothers invited their own mothers, giving us three generations with which to work and explore. It was an international affair with women flying in from South America and Europe to join us. We received a fair amount of press coverage, which included interviews on cable channels and *Newsday*, a review from *NY Magazine*, and an invitation to appear on *The Gayle King Show*. We also published an academic article for the *Group Psychotherapy Journal*.

My mother, Leah, and I led versatile and engaging workshops; many women were fascinated by our own dynamic and relationship. As the group's facilitators, we worked together very well, partly because we approached the topic from differing viewpoints and approaches. Leah was an introverted, Belgian-born woman who escaped the horrors of the Holocaust and came to the United States when she was nine years old. She became a trained psychoanalyst and specialist in group work. As her American born daughter, I graduated from Columbia University with degrees in Counseling and Organizational Psychology. I found ways to emulate my mother's strengths while developing a style that was distinct and different. My mother and I were able to hold our workshops because I chose a career path that was similar to hers -- while her focus was on general counseling, mine was on career counseling. We could each bring our own special elements into the mother-daughter workshops, which allowed women to open doors in their relationships with their mothers and to make room for striking progress.

The work with my mother marked one of the most intense and meaningful professional interludes in both our lives. I remember our deep discussions after every workshop to process issues that arose during the meetings, and their impact not only on our clients but on our own relationship. Sadly, our work slowed down and then came to a halt when my mother was diagnosed with stage-four ovarian cancer. While she still conducted a few workshops, the mother-daughter ones became too painful for me to continue. Whether I wanted to consciously admit it or not, I knew that the disease would take her away from me too soon.

In April 2004, my mother lost her battle with cancer. For almost a decade following my mother's death, I stepped away from the mother-daughter workshops and instead focused on my career counseling practice while also working in the Human Resources department at The New School. In the 26 years since starting my clinical career counseling practice, I have helped hundreds of people who have struggled with some aspect of career indecision. They come to me with their unhappiness and seek my support in identifying new career paths, navigating the workplace, or figuring out how they can stop their anxiety and/or depression from getting in the way of their lives and careers.

In the years following my mother's death, while I've never stopped reflecting on the mother-daughter relationship and our amazing work together, I started to notice the strong connection between women's career issues and their relationships with their mothers. What was especially fascinating to me was that there were patterns in the types of problems women were experiencing and how they related to the mother-daughter relationship. When I ask women clients about their relationships with their mothers, they usually seem surprised or confused. They don't think their careers have anything to do with their moms but once the conversation takes off, I can see how their faces light up in astonishment when a connection has been made.

I'm ready to resume the work my mother and I started twenty-plus years ago; just like back then, I'm ready to add my special perspective on the topic. This book is in honor and in memory of my mother. It is to continue the work I started with her; to continue to fill a need for the daughters who are still navigating their lives and trying to understand how this most powerful relationship shaped their decisions and choices. It is taking my work with my mother and making it my own, exactly what adult daughters need to do.

When this happens for you, you may find yourself more satisfied at work, relating better not only with coworkers but with your mom too. What better day to start living happier than today? Some of the tips that I've provided in this book may resonate with you. Some might not. That's okay. There's a girl inside of each of us. Depending on the triggers, she has the potential in different moments to be an Ivy, Maverick, Butterfly, Copycat or Bootstrap daughter. The purpose of reading *What's Mom Still Got To Do With It?* is to raise awareness of our consistent patterns of behavior. The goal is to explore these patterns and allow the process of healing to begin. You don't have to change everything after reading this book. It took many years to get to where you are today, so it won't be an overnight effort to move you into something new. However, women can find the motivation to make positive changes and leave regret behind at any age. My hope is that all daughters will have their answers to, "What's Mom still got to do with it?", and will be able to move forward for a life they have dreamed about and which they deserve.

Acknowledgments

This book is the result of years of studying the relationship between mothers and daughters, their dynamics, and women's career issues. I am deeply grateful for the professional opportunities I have had in my life to date, and, for the support, inspiration, wisdom, and knowledge I have gained from so many people. I could not have written *What's Mom Still Got To Do With It?* without the huge support from the wonderful people I'm lucky to call my family, friends, mentors, colleagues, and peers.

First and foremost, I want to thank Annie Wong for the five years that she dedicated to this project. Without her, there would be no book. Annie has been my writer, sounding board, and my voice when I couldn't find the words to express myself. Thank you for the invaluable gift of putting my vision into words and for being a truly exceptional writer, colleague, and friend. Marilyn Elias, our content editor, was a great resource with extremely valuable contributions. I am so grateful to Jean Shipos, for her amazing and generous copyediting work. Thank you to my resourceful and creative team of advisors: Robert Fazio and Alexandra Cherasia for your amazing photography and website development; Brian Olson, Jared Kelner, and Michelle Brody for all of your wisdom and advice on self-publishing.

My gratitude goes to my immediate and extended family for the countless ways in which they supported me: Jack, Ezra and Nathaniel, you have been listening to my ideas for years and believed that it would truly happen one day. I am blessed being the mother of two wonderful sons and will therefore always know more about the powerful mother-daughter dynamic from a daughter's point of view. To my husband Jack, who is always a cheerleader, who believed in me and is always so proud of my work and accomplishments. I truly appreciate your generosity with your time and also your support for the time the book took me away from us. Thank you for listening to my inspirations and ideas and helping me channel them. Your contributions were invaluable and you knew just how much advice to offer. You truly make me better than I would be without you. Thank you to my dad Bernie, for your unconditional support, and for doing your best to be mother, father, grandmother and grandfather to all of us since Mom died. Thank you for reading my articles, supporting me and believing in this book. Thank you to my loving sister, Sharon, my awesome brother, Jonathan, and their families for: not just being my siblings but good friends as well; our shared experiences; keeping Mom alive in our hearts; and, keeping us a cohesive unit. To the other amazing women in my family: my sisters-in-law, Tracy and Lori, thank you for your constant encouragement of me and this book.

Thank you to all of my friends and to the incredible community of women who shared their experiences with me. I appreciate your stories about your mothers and daughters, quotes and anything else I asked for, whether it was by text, Facebook, interviews or in person: Cindy R.; Fanny H.; Wendy P.; Cindy G.; Tracy T.; Susan M.; Amy S.; Marla F.; Lora S.; Lisa P.H.; Karen A.; Stephanie B.; Tracy F.; Meryl C.; Cary S.; Jodi Y.; Liti H.; Norma L.; Rebecca H.; Elisabeth S.P.; Suzanne S.; Yael S.; Lindsey S.; Brianna Y.; Renee R.; Anita Y.; Marcy F.; Vera C.; Bridget R.; Julia S.J.; Ellen Z. and all the women who shared beautiful pieces of themselves throughout the years -- thank you for trusting me with your stories and for participating in in-depth interviews. A special thank you to Amy Schafer, Stephanie Basta, Jodi Young and Merryl Centeno for reading chapters, helping with the website text and supporting this project in countless, generous ways.

I am grateful to all of my dear professional colleagues. Every woman should be so lucky to have intimate professional relationships with like-minded colleagues. In particular, I want to acknowledge and thank the women in my clinical supervision group, my wonderful colleagues at CDSN (Career Development Specialists Network) in New York City and those who I met through NCDA. To my colleagues and friends: Dr. Ilene Zwirn; Dr. Lauren Saler; Cary Sellers; Tracy Fink; Carol Vecchio; Dorothy Firman; and, Patricia DiMango. I can't thank you enough for your wisdom along the way, taking the time to read the book and offering your feedback for the cover and website.

Thank you to: my clients; the participants in the mother-daughter workshops that my mother and I conducted; and, former strangers for giving me the privilege of being part of your lives and for revealing your deep realities about your relationships, careers and lives. I have such deep gratitude to: Carol Cantrell; Liz Ross; Judith Bristol; and, Rose Lederman -- my own bosses, mentors, surrogate mothers and wise advisors. I would not be who I am today without the amazing opportunities you gave me. Your guidance, love, and support have shaped who I am, personally and professionally.

Finally, I want to thank my mother, Leah, who not only gave me life, love, and a belief in myself; but she was also a true role model for living one's best life, modelling gratefulness for all that life has to offer and she showed me that I can do anything to which I set my mind. Mom, you live inside of me and I know exactly what you think about this accomplishment.

About Ilana

Ilana Tolpin Levitt, M.A., M.Ed., L.P.C., L.M.H.C., is a clinical career counselor with over 26 years of experience in private practice in New York City and Central New Jersey. She is the 2013 recipient of the Outstanding Career Practitioner Award from the National Career Development Association. As a Licensed Mental Health Counselor, Ilana's focus with many clients is a deep exploration of the psychological roots that impact career development and workplace dysfunction. In addition, Ilana is the Director of Employee Development and Organizational Effectiveness at The New School in New York City. Many of her clients struggle with anxiety, depression and other internal barriers that interfere with their success. For over a decade, Ilana ran mother-daughter relationship workshops with her mother who was a psychoanalyst. *What's Mom Still Got To Do With It?* integrates her knowledge and experience about mother-daughter relationships with her expertise in career development, and, human resources. She lives in New Jersey with her husband, two teenaged sons and two golden retrievers.

For more information, visit www.whatsmomthebook.com.

39210596R00091

Made in the USA
Middletown, DE
08 January 2017